Parenting Teens

Parenting Guide to Help Your Chi d Become His or Her Best Self

(A Guide for Parents to Raising Independent)

Carlos Cunningham

Published by Rob Miles

© Carlos Cunningham

All Rights Reserved

Parenting Teens: Parenting Guide to Help Your Child Become His or Her Best Self (A Guide for Parents to Raising Independent)

ISBN 9781990084447

All rights reserved. No part of this guide may be reproduced in any form without permission in writing from the publisher except in the case of brief quotations embodied in critical articles or reviews.

Legal & Disclaimer

The information contained in this book is not designed to replace or take the place of any form of medicine or professional medical advice. The information in this book has been provided for educational and entertainment purposes only.

The information contained in this book has been compiled from sources deemed reliable, and it is accurate to the best of the Author's knowledge; however, the Author cannot guarantee its accuracy and validity and cannot be held liable for any errors or omissions. Changes are periodically made to this book. You must consult your doctor or get professional medical advice before using any of the suggested remedies, techniques, or information in this book.

Upon using the information contained in this book, you agree to hold harmless the Author from and against any damages, costs, and expenses, including any legal fees potentially resulting from the application of any of the information provided by this guide. This disclaimer applies to any damages or injury caused by the use and application, whether directly or indirectly, of any advice or information presented, whether for breach of contract, tort, negligence, personal injury, criminal intent, or under any other cause of action.

You agree to accept all risks of using the information presented inside this book. You need to consult a professional medical practitioner in order to ensure you are both able and healthy enough to participate in this program.

Table of Contents

INTRODUCTION 1

CHAPTER 1: WELCOME TO TANTRUM CITY 3

CHAPTER 2: HOW TO ENCOURAGE LEARNING IN YOUR CHILD 9

CHAPTER 3: WAYS TO DEVELOP A PARENTAL SUPPORT NETWORK IN ORDER TO BE A MORE EFFECTIVE PARENT. 15

CHAPTER 4: CAT PROOFING THE CRADLE 24

CHAPTER 5: HOW DO YOU KNOW IF YOUR CHILD IS PREDISPOSED TO BE ENTREPRENEURIAL? 37

CHAPTER 6: PAUSE AND REFLECT 46

CHAPTER 7: EASY DISCIPLINE TACTICS 51

CHAPTER 8: HOW TO BE A POSITIVE SINGLE PARENT 56

CHAPTER 9: LEARNING THE SKILLS OF PARENTING 63

CHAPTER 10: INABILITY FOR UNDIVIDED ATTENTION 70

CHAPTER 11 74

CHAPTER 12: DISCIPLINE POSITIVELY 80

CHAPTER 13: DISCIPLINE IN A POSITIVE WAY 87

CHAPTER 14: BENEFITS OF BEING A SINGLE PARENT 94

CHAPTER 15: FOLLOWING THROUGH ON PROMISES 97

CHAPTER 16: GETTING RID OF THE GUILT 101

CHAPTER 17: HOW TO SOLVE PROBLEMS THAT ARISE ... 107

CHAPTER 18: TIPS YOU CAN USE 122

CHAPTER 19: KEEPING SOME NORMALCY FOR THE CHILDREN AFTER A DIVORCE 128

CHAPTER 20: CAN IT BE THAT MY CHILD IS A VICTIM OF ABUSE? 135

CHAPTER 21: THE IMPORTANCE OF RELAXATION 146

CHAPTER 22: BE A GOOD LISTENER AND LET YOUR CHILD TELL THEIR SIDE 151

CHAPTER 23: KEEP PROMISES 154

CHAPTER 24: TALKING TO KIDS ABOUT DIVORCE 158

CHAPTER 25: SMART KIDS ARE ADAPTABLE 165

CHAPTER 26: PREVENT CHILDHOOD ILLNESS WITH THE HELP OF YOUR DOCTOR 180

CHAPTER 27: IDENTIFY YOUR TRIGGERS 186

CHAPTER 28: START PARENTING MORE EFFECTIVELY 191

CONCLUSION 199

Introduction

Being a parent is not an easy job. As someone rightly put it "Your job as a parent is not only to provide food, clothing, shelter, and a safe and loving environment for your child, it is also your DUTY as a parent to be aware of your child's natural talents i.e. (athletic, musical, intellectual etc.), and to do everything in your power to develop & cultivate those attributes."

As a parent, you are responsible for instilling faith in your children as well as helping your children realize that within them lies a unique power; a power they need to unleash and exploit so that they can be their best.

Moreover, it is your duty as a parent to develop a growth mindset in a child; a growth mindset is a type of mindset that gives an individual strength to believe in themselves, and understand that they can enhance and amplify whatever capabilities they have. This is only possible when you pay attention to your children, their needs, and are there for them.

If you want to help your children unlock their true abilities and talents, this guide will prove to be of great benefit to you. It is aimed at equipping you with the knowledge and expertise required to help your child unleash his or her amazing inner power.

Thanks again for downloading this book, I hope you enjoy it!

Chapter 1: Welcome To Tantrum City

Welcome to the stage of early childhood! This is an exciting time for your children and for parents as well. Your children are trying to learn and know everything at a really fast pace – sometimes it gets too fast for the poor parents. Toddlers are trying to learn more about this world that they are living in and they are also learning new things about themselves. On top of that, they are also trying to learn to socialize with other people, which include grownups and other kids as well.

Sometimes all this excitement can eventually lead to a meltdown for your child. For the most part, when children don't get what they want they throw a tantrum. Of course there are many different causes but that one is right at the top of the list.

Sometimes a tantrum isn't just a young child's problem. Sometimes new parents also get frustrated and don't know what to do. They don't understand why their children are behaving the way they do during a tantrum. Some parents fail to cope with the situation, especially if it causes an embarrassment. At that point they tend to punish a young child because they threw a tantrum.

Guess what. It doesn't work, doesn't it? Resorting to punishments, light or otherwise only encourages your child to keep doing what they are doing – especially in public. Do you remember a time when you were in a public place like a church or a supermarket? There was this something that your child said or wanted but you just brushed it off or said no.

A short time later your child's countenance looks a little different. Some kids' faces can change in shade (some become quite reddish) when they're furious. Some kids pound their fists, some start stomping, hitting, kicking, biting, or even holding their breath. Some kids just cry – these are pretty common tantrum techniques they try.

These episodes are often quite embarrassing especially when there are other people who gander at the spectacle. Sometimes you wish you can just hide somewhere no one can see you. To any parent who has gone through these scenarios – Welcome to tantrum city!

The Mechanics of a Tantrum and How They Work

A toddler's tantrums usually aren't a big deal when they happen only once in a while. Some parents are truly fortunate never to have experienced them at all. Tantrums only become a problem when they become more frequent than usual. However, do take note that temper tantrums are pretty common among children ages 1 to 4.

Kids at that age are still trying to learn how to communicate how they feel. They sometimes just don't know the words or sometimes they just don't know how to properly express themselves. Studies show that 50% of all kids will throw a tantrum about once a week. They either do that as a protest to whatever control or decision you made for them or they do that to show how frustrated they are.

Clinical psychologist Ray Levy explains that tantrums are a fact of early childhood. Toddlers are still developing their coping skills (they're learning so give them time). It's their way of expressing a feeling they don't understand or know how to say – so they just tend to go on and lose it (i.e. blow off steam).

Dr. Levy also states that almost all tantrums result from the fact the child didn't get what he wanted. Kids at a younger age (i.e. from 1 to 2 years old) don't know how to tell you that they want a diaper change, or they want milk, or they want you to give them their favorite toy. They throw a tantrum to get your attention and to expedite matters.

Older tots (i.e. ages 3 to 4 years) have learned to assert what they want. They tend to be testy. They have learned to be somewhat more autoromous and assertive. If mommy or daddy doesn't give them what they want, then they throw a tantrum just to see if you will give them what they want.

Why Can't You Reason with a Child Throwing a Temper Tantrum?

Minnesota pediatrician Jay Hoecker explains why you can't reason with a child who is throwing a tantrum. Hoecker explains that a child throwing a tantrum can't be reasoned with simply because that part of their brain that is used for making decisions (i.e. the frontal cortex) has been overridden. What overrides their ability to listen? The answer is simple – their emotions.

The child's emotions have taken over thus their reasoning skills have taken a backseat. Experts often compare tantrum with the condition of someone who is already drowning. You can't teach that person to swim — their minds have been clouded. Their ONLY concern is to get to safety. That is why they grab hold of anyone or anything within their reach just to survive.

The same is true with the child. They won't listen. You can't reason with them while they're in that state. You can only reason with a child when the panic and stress is over.

Chapter 2: How To Encourage Learning In Your Child

Apart from fun and games, a smart kid should be nurtured from an early age by encouraging his/her brain development on all areas of the child's life. For this to happen, you need to exercise both sides of your child's brain; the right and left sides. The former functions is logic, reasoning and language, and the latter's function is creativity and arts. We will look at how you can encourage learning in your child to ensure that you nurture their smartness.

Use of Cognitive Development Skills

One of the ways to nurture creativity in your child is through cognitive development skills, which develop because of problem solving situations, whether activated by you the parent, or through peer influence. When your child is growing, during the first eighteen months, he/she experiences difficulty relating with symbols. However, when they reach their second year, thinking in images develops. Similarly, when your child is young, their attention span is random. However, at the end of the second year, this changes and their attention span increases dramatically. They can control their attention span and will hold on to something that grasps their attention until they are satisfied.

Generally, cognitive development skills are essentially meant to help a child improve their decision-making, abstract thinking and concentration abilities. However, since children between the age of two and seven learn through hands on and concrete methods, the only way to go about it is through direct play and interaction. A good activity to encourage development of these skills is through age appropriate puzzles. These are fun and encourage problem solving skills, and critical thinking. You can also use simple board games to promote your child's problem solving skills and teach them how to follow directions. Games and puzzles are also a great way to teach your child categorization for example arrangement into group by color, size and type. It also plays a major role in enforcing concentration and memory skills. As your child continues to grow, the objectives and rules of the game change and become more interesting. You can then introduce such games as checkers at this time. You can find these and many classic games at the store, but you can also easily make your own. As your child grows, they can benefit a lot from make believe.

Throughout this period, training your kids to place themselves in imaginary situations and learning how to deal with different situations can help stretch their imagination and improve their problem solving skills. While most parents do not make sense of such pretend games as acting like a princess or dinosaur, these can still help your child a lot. In essence, the point here is to encourage creativity through problem solving scenarios. Your kids will be more inclined to play when one or two of you parents are involved. In some cases, children usually tend to have a set of hidden rules that seem so obvious to them but may not be as susceptible to you. However, as long as they are not screaming or making menace, it should still be encouraged. When they have run out of ideas, you can then try out your own.

As a parent, your make believe scenarios can either be simpler than the children's to encourage creativity, or they can be more complex when you want to teach specific topics. Some of the themes you can use in your make believe include caring and nurturing scenes like playing good guy against bad guy, or acting like a wild animal. In addition, be sure to diversify on various topics in order to teach on different areas of life. As long as the games are not violent or hurtful, they are okay. However, since children tend to learn a lot from make believe, you will have to be creative as time goes by. Some children tend to be very imitative of their parents, and are sometimes seen to imitate what their parents are doing. As such, you can capitalize on this and use this interest to enlist them on a couple of basic chores. While you may find chores monotonous to do, this could be an important learning platform for your kids. For instance, your toddler may arrange the laundry according to color and type in different piles, while an older preschooler may help with the dishes and meals. However, make sure you make a clear distinction of the term helping and the actual act of doing the chores. While it is in order to correct your child's mistake, make sure that you do not scold them for making a mistake. If possible, wait until the child is settled and calm before raising the topic. The main purpose of these activities is to enhance family bonding, provide space for learning and improve their self-esteem.

Chapter 3: Ways To Develop A Parental Support Network In Order To Be A More Effective Parent

The Need For A Support Network Today

I always tell parents that one of the most important parts of modern parenting is putting together a support network that works. Too many parents try to be completely self-sufficient. However, all parents have heard of the idea that it takes a village to raise a child. This is common folk wisdom that modern parents should take to heart. Nothing can destroy happy parenting like the stress of being forced to handle everything in isolation.

The current situation involving a two-parent family raising a child purely independently is rare historically. In fact, grandparents often participated strongly in the raising of children, leaving young adults to do more work for the entire group in early human societies. Even in many cultures around the world today, the whole family helps with the new baby and the kids. At the very least, parents are not expected to do it all themselves.

Too many parents are forced to do the work of at least three people themselves. This situation has only gotten worse with time. Kids used to be able to walk to school by themselves. Today, parents who let their kids do this can get arrested for child neglect even if the kid gets there and back safely.

People can't parent alone, but the expectation in modern society is that they will. Even people who are not single parents often functionally act as if they are. It's rare for two parents to spend an equal amount of quality time with their kids. Moms usually spend twice as much time with kids as dads. This situation varies a lot with same-sex parents, but truthfully, the responsibility is too much even for a lot of couples that perfectly share everything.

Working With Family And Friends

Some people are lucky enough to have a lot of established family and friends in their local areas. I've found that the people who already had a lot of close friends and family members will typically make the transition to parenthood much easier than a lot of other people.

There's a longstanding stereotype that a lot of mothers struggle with their mothers-in-law when it comes to raising their kids. Women who are not close to their mothers-in-law are unlucky in that way. There are plenty of women who genuinely are close to their mothers-in-law and their mothers, and their mothers are often happy to help them babysit, get groceries, make ends meet, or otherwise handle many of the tough tasks associated with parenthood.

This situation is more common with Millennial parents. Many Millennials have never been able to afford to live outside of their parents' homes in general because of the scarcity of jobs for the Millennial generation, the rising cost of living, and the level of debt that most Millennial parents have. On the plus side, a lot of Millennial parents already have a solid support network when they decide to become parents themselves. Of course, some Millennial parents might be worse off than most other parents of other generational cohorts, because they have even less money and no support network.

Some people are not lucky enough to have mothers, mothers-in-law, and other family members who are hugely supportive. However, some of them might still be willing to help out sometimes. I would advise most people to consider the nature of the conflicts that they have with some family members. If the family member in question is abusive, then breaking off contact with him or her might be the safest thing to do for everyone. However, mothers-in-law who are just a bit pushy in the stereotypical sitcom sense might still be valuable allies in a world where parenting just keeps on getting more and more difficult all the time.

I know that people might think that moving next door to their parents sounds like it isn't worth it. However, depending on how many kids are involved and what the parents are like, it actually might be for some people. New parents should never underestimate the sheer difficulties of being a parent today. Having someone to call when your kid gets sick or having a person around who can bring around dinner when you can't get home from work can truly make all the difference in the world.

Some family members might be willing to move in order to support new family members with kids. There are some close friends who might be willing to do the same thing. One way or another, having people like this in your life is something that is so helpful that it is worth it to at least explore some of the options involved.

Support Networks For Parents Without Family Or Established Friends

Parents who don't have a lot of family members or friends will have to build these relationships from scratch. One of the good things about being a parent is that a lot of people more or less are willing to bring a person into a sort of honorary 'mommy club' or 'daddy club' as a result. There are lots of different meetup groups that people can find online that are just for moms, dads, or both. Members of these meetup groups will often babysit for free. They will tend to give each other supportive tips. It's a great place for emotional support and for tangible financial and social support.

Parental meetup groups are especially important for the people who are parenting alone and the people who have had to move to an unfamiliar area. Lots of people move for a new job today. This can cause people to be displaced from their support networks. Parents need support networks more than anyone. Fortunately, other parents are aware of this, and they have taken the liberty of establishing themselves on meetup websites.

It should be relatively easy to find them. While model train enthusiasts and German language clubs might be more common in some areas than others, there are parents everywhere. Even in relatively remote areas, it should be possible to find some meetup groups for parents.

Parents with new kids might have a hard time doing any of the work necessary involved with getting together a support group. It is certainly a better idea to try to get as much of this work done beforehand. However, the Internet has made it easier for even the busiest of new parents to make this work. Even communicating with people on meetup websites from home can help to establish some parental friendships early in the process. Even busy new parents might be able to work on some positive relationships from a distance, and they might eventually be able to go to a meetup meeting. They might even be able to get other new parents to help them from there.

Parents Need Friends

Of course, even beyond all of the benefits of having parent friends, I really think it needs to be emphasized that parents need to have friends for their own sake. When you hear about all of the worst parts of parenting from a lot of modern parents, one word comes up over and over again: isolation.

New parents are shocked by the fact that they feel like they are completely out off from the world. This seems to apply to working parents as well as stay-at-home parents, actually, especially if those parents are work-at-home parents. Going to work and then coming home to the kids doesn't leave a lot of time for socializing. Chasing after the kids all day can leave people drained. Some people will never see their old friends again.

This loss of friendship is never something that parents should embrace as an inevitable part of parenthood, and yet so many of them do today. It's become a lament of the modern parent. Parents will go online and compose long essays about how they miss their friends, but they know that as parents, their time to have fun with their friends is gone. It's amazing that some people will still wonder why they are so unhappy after they've decided that, among other things, they have to give up on their friends.

Happy parents have friends. That's all there is to it. Parents make time today in order to get their kids to countless activities. They can certainly find a way to have friends. It's also a good idea to have parent friends. While you can have childfree-by-choice friends as well, they're not going to understand the fact that you have to cancel an outing because of Lisa's fever.

Your mom or dad friend will as a matter of course. Your mom or dad friend will also be better at offering advice and favors when it comes to childcare, and your childfree friend might not be willing or able to babysit or anything of that nature. If you try to cultivate and nurture friendly relationships with other parents, you will be that much closer to happiness in no time.

Chapter 4: Cat Proofing The Cradle

Undoubtedly, we have all observed the following curiosity.Children, especially the very young, equate attention with love.Much like a child's stomach will tell her if her 'food tank' is full, a child's heart will tell her if her 'love tank' is full.In this, they have an unconscious (yet felt) need to fill their 'love tank.'In other words, whether a child knows it or not, she will seek to gain a certain amount of love daily- in the form of attention- from those closest to her. A baby, who is hungry, cries. A child, who needs love, cries out.

We, as parents, are the main suppliers of this 'felt' commodity. If the child's caregiver ignores this need, the child will spend an exorbitant amount of energy doing whatever necessity requires to receive that love- in the form of attention. At this point the child is no longer concerned with whether that attention is positive or negative. The child senses emotional starvation. Such behavior is consistent with a physically starving child. If she is truly starving, she no longer cares if the milk is sour or the meat is crawling with maggots. A starving child is simply glad to have something to eat.

The reality of absent parenting is that the whole family experience becomes helter-skelter. The more a parent neglects to provide the attention her child needs, the more the child acts out in order to fill her 'love tank' (even with sour milk). The more the child acts out, the more defeated the parent becomes and the less likely the parent is to give the child the attention for which the child truly- yet unconsciously- longs.Typically the tension in the home rises, and rises, and rises.

Observers see all to often, the child as the issue in the home.After all, it is the child who is throwing food, throwing herself in the floor or refusing to clean up the mess she made.Society makes it far too easy to blame the issue on the child in the form of a disorder or other defect.After all, it is socially acceptable to simply have your child labeled and treated by professionals.We have a drug for everything.We tell our children don't do drugs, and the minute one of them has something that can be labeled 'a problem,' we prescribe a drug to 'treat' it.In other words, we tend to gravitate toward treating the child as the problem as a society instead of looking at the sociological challenges within the family unit first.

On the other end of the spectrum are children whose love tanks are consistently full.My personal observation has been that these children appear to be more intelligent.Yet I know in my heart of hearts that this just simply cannot be true.As I continued to observe, a different conclusion surfaced: children with consistently full love tanks do not have to expend emotional and mental energy to obtain the necessary amount of love, each day, in the form of attention.Therefore, these kids can spend the same energy that emotionally starving children spend to obtain any form of attention they can from their caregivers, exploring their world.Thus, children with full love tanks expand their knowledge exponentially and in doing so, carry the illusion of possessing greater mental aptitude.

Maybe to you, dear reader, the children I just described might as well be fairy tales.In your world I might as well be discussing the finer points of Peter and

Wendy, Christopher Robin, or Strawberry Shortcake.Yet such children truly do exist, maybe within the circle of people that you know.However, if you do not have the time to fill the love tanks of your own children, how would you ever have the time to observe children who respond to their parents in a more positive way?Some of us are just way too busy.

I worked in a mall, a few years back that was doing a remodel.The management company had ordered some exotic Italian tile for the new restroom facilities they were constructing.The contractor under ordered the tile and the whole project ended up being delayed by more than a month.The reason was truly 'un-American.'The Italian company, who manufactured the decorative tile, took the entire month of August off each and every year.

Everyone on this side of the Atlantic seemed dumbfounded by the idea.Yet Europeans, I am told, scratch their heads over how much we Americans work.Europeans, it seems, work to live.We Americans, on the other hand, appear to live to work.We tend to derive our self worth from our careers.Yet most of us would regurgitate, on request, the old adage, 'that what I do is not who I am.'Seventy-hour workweeks provide strong evidence of our self-deceit.Allow me to prove it to you.

There are 168 hours in a week.If we work 70 hours, that leaves 98 hours for the rest of our existence.Even if we only average 6 hours a night sleeping, that takes another 42 hours a week away, leaving us with 56.Let us say that the process of eating (preparation or travel, consumption, clean up) requires another 2 hours, on average, per day.Now we are left with 42 hours to divide amongst the rest of our life.Personal time, such as working out, church, playing golf, etc... most likely eats up another 10 hours a week.Then there are the chores around the house that need to be done (yard work, paying bills, trips to the store for this or that, etc...).Even if this only takes 8 hours out of your week, you are only left with a single day (24 hours) for your wife and kids.

The question we should ask ourselves is how much do we actually need?Storage facilities are full of extra furniture, clothes and other items that we tell ourselves we will use again... someday.With gas prices fluctuating the way they are, we are paying, more than ever, for those oversized status symbols known as luxury SUVs.Our houses are larger than ever, but have less laughter and fellowship in them than they did twenty years ago simply because we do not have the time to spend in them.The larger our houses get, the less homes we have in America.

The issue, it seems, was posted for most to see in the pages of the latest Harry Potter Novel, Harry Potter and the Deathly Hallows (Scholastic; 2007).In it, J.K. Rowling reminds us of an ancient ideal:

'Where your treasure is, there is your heart.'In the good ol' USA we like to say, 'take a look at where you spend your money.'But can we agree there is a more valuable treasure that we all have in limited supply?

That treasure is time.Take the richest man in the world who is lying on his deathbed.At the point where the doctors have concurred that there is nothing else they can do for him, all of his assets will not buy him another week, another day, another hour, another minute.Time cannot be bought at any price.

Children understand this.The point of the Richard Prior/Jackie Gleason comedy classic, The Toy (Columbia Pictures; 1982), was that having all the toys in the world did nothing to make Eric Bates feel valued.What the child needed more than anything was his father's time and attention.Richard Prior's character, Jack Brown, convinced U. S. Bates of this before the movie's end.This principle that we laughed about in movie theaters in 1982 is still universal today.Time is the greatest treasure on earth.That treasure is the only treasure our children truly need.

So we have to ask ourselves: where does how we spend our time say about where our heart is?Maybe, dear reader, you are feeling validated right now.You need to know that the sacrifices you are making to have more time with your kids is the right thing to do.My wife and I have been fortunate to be able to make the sacrifice of her leaving the work force and staying home with our children up until now.We see it as the best private education money cannot buy.Since she is worth at least $50,000 a year in the corporate world, that is the price we pay willingly for this service to our children.If dollars are what drives you, this equates to us 'spending' (up to this point) nearly a half of a million dollars for our children to have the best 'nanny/teacher' in the world for the two of them.Many of you reading this (especially moms) can now put a dollar amount on the pride you feel for the sacrifice you are making for your children.You truly have the greatest career money cannot buy.Do not let anyone, through word or gesture, tell you otherwise.

Others of you, dear reader, do not know how to feel.One finds his or herself conflicted.One wants to retort that you have worked hard for your kids to have the things you feel they need.You have a nice, big house, in a good neighborhood, with excellent schools.Your children have eaten some of the best chicken nuggets money can buy.Birthdays are never disappointments.Even ponies are not beyond your means.Sadly, what one is actually saying is that even when your children are closest to you, they are not close to you.

Feng Shui, the Chinese art of arranging the architecture and furniture in your life to achieve a desired objective, encourages residential design that keeps secondary bedrooms in close proximity to the master.Feng Shui Masters say this promotes family unity.Yet tour new home models (especially the larger floor plans) over the last two decades and you will find that many designers go as far as to put the children's bedrooms on a separate floor from that of the master.We are a nation who now prides itself on our individual isolation- I mean independence.Experts tell us that better than seventy percent of all communication is nonverbal.What are our children hearing from us when we buy a house whose architect ensures their space is as far from our own personal space as we can possibly make it?

Are we not all realizing, as the economy takes a nosedive, that people are what we should value most?The way we show them value is with our time.Toss the gym membership and take a bike ride as a family.Eat at home.You cannot possibly equal the caloric intake you will receive at any of your favorite restaurants.But most of all, find a way to spend less time at work.Most executive positions could easily support two families (or more).Maybe those positions should provide for two families (or more).Two heads are better than one.It is only logical to believe that two people splitting a seventy-hour job in half could do a far better job spending forty hours each.

You may not be able to go to Aruba every year, but you will never miss another milestone in your child's life.Those milestones are precious treasures that can only be acquired by being a part of them.You will, as well, have the time to spend building relationships with the people around you and watch them have a positive effect on the men and women your children can become.You will not miss your child's first homerun or touchdown.You will not miss your child's role in the school play.Most of all, your children will not miss you.Of course, with all the new found time you will have with your children, we must make sure we know how best to communicate with them.

Chapter 5: How Do You Know If Your Child Is Predisposed To Be Entrepreneurial?

Are they capable of it?

To see if your child is capable of becoming an entrepreneur, you need to ask yourself a question: who do we call an entrepreneur? Don't search Wikipedia, it includes only legal aspects of the term. We, present or future parents, care mostly about an Entrepreneur with a capital E - a true company owner, who's born to run a successful business, who's full of ideas, and not afraid of challenges. But does your child need to run a company? Absolutely not! In this e-book I'd like to encourage parents to raise children who have entrepreneurial traits, but don't have to actually become entrepreneurs. The idea is to make children capable of managing a team, their finances, taking challenges, and coming up with great ideas in the future.

To see if your child is capable of becoming an entrepreneur, you need to ask yourself a question: who do we call an entrepreneur? Don't search Wikipedia, it includes only legal aspects of the term. We, present or future parents, care mostly about an Entrepreneur with a capital E - a true company owner, who's born to run a successful business, who's full of ideas, and not afraid of challenges. But does your child need to run a company? Absolutely not! In this e-book I'd like to encourage parents to raise children who have entrepreneurial traits, but don't have to actually become entrepreneurs. The idea is to make children capable of managing a team, their finances, taking challenges, and coming up with great ideas in the future.

If a child's brain worked as yours.

Let's go back in time. You're looking at your little self. You're great at crawling, sometimes you can even stand up, holding on to your mother's legs or a table. This week you're going to take your first steps. What happens now? Inspired by big people surrounding you, also called adults, you use your hands to support yourself, and lift your bum to slowly stand up. Not for long, however. You push yourself off the floor too hard and fall down, so be grateful for a diaper that softens your fall. You think to yourself:

"Okay... I failed once, so I'll try again, but now I won't push off myself so hard".

You start over. Second time, the fall isn't so quick, and you even manage to take two steps. Taking the third step, you confuse the left leg with the right one, and you fall on the floor again. You think:

"It's more complicated than I thought. But I want to walk so badly! By crawling I can't reach where I want! I'll try again!"

You try, and this time you take a few more steps, but you encounter an obstacle: a high-pile rug, and, obviously, you trip on it.

Your little self learns how to walk by trying three times and failing each time. You're not surrounded by people who, like you, are learning to walk, and all you see is big people with long legs, and they all can walk already. Imagine then, that you, as a baby, thought:

"Okay, I see. Everything tells me one thing: I'm not capable of walking, not everyone needs to walk, and apparently, other children are better at this. I'll just be crawling then, because I'm great at that".

This is the natural instinct of an entrepreneur.

The situation above describes what would happen if a child's brain worked as most adults' brains. What I tried to show by the described scene is a human natural tendency to face challenges and take risks. People are born to learn how to walk even if they have to try and fail a thousand times. Neanderthals would take risks everyday when they came out their caves and hunt animals. Therefore, if either you or educational system haven't destroyed this natural instinct yet, your child isn't afraid of challenges and is predisposed to become a great entrepreneur.

Children are just born to do it. They don't give up and know that they can learn everything, even if the circumstances suggest something different.

The older children are, the more they lose their ability to learn on their own. Or, in other words, children start to follow what adults do. In this field, we should rather learn from our children.

Look closely at your son or daughter.

If you're still think that there are people who are better at becoming entrepreneurs and those who will never achieve that, despite my short story, I'll explain.

Read the following descriptions and see if at least one suits your child. Which one best describes your child?

1. Your child is more mature than their age implies.

You look at your child and you see this sparkle in their eye. You notice that your child can associate facts and think in an abstract way, is perceptive and recognizes not only items and events, but also abstract concepts. Moreover, your child is great at drawing conclusions.

2. Your child constantly comes up with ideas.

Not always is your child going to make their ideas come to life, but they're always full of them. A new fantastic game? Your child has already come up with it. The same goes for the new use of an ordinary item that you'd never use in that particular way, and even a new position to pick the nose - yes, it also can be innovative :)

3. Your child understands the concept of money.

Your child is interested in the concept of money much earlier than their peers, or has no problems with understanding the difference between coins and bills or the concept of giving change.

4. Your child is interested in money and material things.

Your daughter not only dresses up her dolls, but also puts a hot tub and a garage in their house. Your son, while playing with building blocks, emphasizes the use of "super lasers" or "new generation devices". He's not satisfied with ordinary things, since he can have everything. Your child more often asks if a thing is cheap or expensive.

5. Your child plays more with adults than peers.

Children are bored in the company of their peers. However, they're excited when they're surrounded by adults, and they'reinterested in various aspects of being an adult.

In order to know that your child is predisposed to become an entrepreneur, you don't have to match any of the above descriptions to them. Your child may become a particular type of an entrepreneur, for example, a typical manager, an economist who has a flair for investments, or a creator full of ideas worth big bucks/a bundle/a lot of money. There are many types of entrepreneurs, and each of them is characterized by a trait which makes it worth investing in your child's proper education. If there is any basis to develop your child's entrepreneurial skills, you should start doing it, and let it be the perfect beginning of your child's education.

Proper education.

Not all adults are capable of becoming entrepreneurs, but all children are. Why? Because they have more potential than all adults together. Children don't lose their abilities and natural predispositions to achieve great things.

Unfortunately, the differences between your child's skills are bigger as the time passes. It's caused by various factors. But one's for sure: don't expect that your child will learn everything in school, because school focuses mostly on a curriculum, tests, exams, and the idea of "good behavior" and "good grades". Therefore, there's no place for developing creativity, or problem-solving, public-speaking and money-saving skills, etc.

Speaking about "proper" education I'm not referring to enrolling your child in a class with a specialized curriculum (for example, focused on economics), or extra English classes. Yes, economic and language knowledge is useful, but it doesn't make anyone an entrepreneur. Your task, dear parents, is to keep natural instincts in your child and to develop new mechanisms useful in their future lives.

Chapter 6: Pause And Reflect

Having children is one of the most tremendous, life-changing decisions anyone can make. It is important to put the necessary amount of thought into it. Prospective parents should consider whether or not they are financially, logistically, and above all, emotionally ready for having children at this stage in their lives. Parents shape their lives around their children, and almost everything fundamentally changes after having kids.

Being a stay-at-home parent effectively requires you to take on the roles of a cook, performer, teacher, custodian, counselor, nurse, and guard while being with your children, and it is difficult for many people to switch between tasks like that. Parenting is a job for generalists, or people who must learn to become generalists. Stay-at-home parents may be in a unique working environment, but they arguably face a more demanding job than most workers. They lose most of their privacy while caring for children, and cannot count on a full night's sleep. Effectively, stay-at-home parents are 'on call' all the time, needed to respond to any emergency. The needs of babies and children will come first, and parents do not have anywhere near as much control of their lives when they are taking care of their children. Also, unlike with most jobs, parents rarely have the option to quit.

Raising children is expensive. There is no getting around that fact, and the costs increase with every child. There are potential tax and other legal benefits available for people with children, and prospective parents should look into them. However, the financial costs are still much higher. Ideally, prospective parents should been in a stable enough financial situation before they seriously consider having children. The costs of raising children do not end after eighteen years, and some parents may continue supporting their children at some level or another for the full duration of their lives. The costs of college educations seem to increase more and more every year, and unless there is a major cultural change in the near future, it is literally never too early to start saving for children's college education.

Working and raising children at the same time is a rewarding, yet very difficult task. It is very difficult for most families in the United States to support a family on a single income. However, childcare often costs more than many people make, particularly women. Working mothers also still face an unfortunate stigma in the workplace. Employers have the bias that working mothers will have few priorities beyond their children, and will be too difficult to promote. The stigma hurts women's earnings. However, the Internet has given stay-at-home mothers and fathers more opportunities to earn money while taking care of their young children. They can write content articles online, do part-time online tutoring, or start blogs and try monetizing them. There are entire job websites for mothers and fathers who work from home, with flexible hours that can allow even someone caring for a one-year-old to earn some extra money. Investigating the available opportunities for parents is important for anyone considering becoming a parent.

People have children for all sorts of reasons. There are some reasons that work out better for both the parents and children than others. Many people, especially those in their late twenties and early thirties, experience tremendous social pressure to have children. Giving into any sort of social pressure is rarely a satisfying experience even if you succeed at doing so adequately. Indeed, social pressures surrounding children do not go away if you do have children. Friends, family, and acquaintances will still be evaluating your parenting performance and lifestyles as parents. It is getting easier than ever, socially and emotionally speaking, for people to lead a non-traditional family life. There is much greater social acceptance for single parents, foster parents, and adoptive parents today than ever before. Moreover, there is less pressure to have children when you are young and late fatherhood and motherhood is starting to become a new normal. People today need not feel pressure to have children according to a certain schedule. Indeed, ideally, people should have children according to their own, personal schedule.

Anyone considering having children should not just consider whether or not they want 'a baby.' Childhood is a temporary state, and each stage of childhood is shorter still. They should also consider raising a toddler, a young child, a preadolescent, and a teenager. One of the joys of childrearing is watching your children grow and develop, and it is important to remember that this is what childrearing is for everyone. Being emotionally ready for each stage of childrearing is important for anyone seriously considering having children.

Chapter 7: Easy Discipline Tactics

Life isn't easy but kids will try your patience. As they grow older they try to stretch their boundaries. Sometimes it works and sometimes it doesn't. When you come in from work and find that your kids are running rampant around the house and generally making themselves nuisances, you do need to have boundaries for all of the kids so that they know that their behavior is not acceptable. One of the best ways that I do this with kids is to be very calm and to explain to the child that the behavior they are exhibiting isn't something I want to deal with after my day of work. I place the child into a room away from the family and the child is not to leave that room until the child is permitted to do so. Other people call this "Time out" but I tend to call it common sense. If you have kids that are arguing and you are not sure who caused the problem, you need to split the kids up and if it means using two quiet spaces then do so.

After twenty minutes of silence, go back into the room and ask the child if he/she is ready to come back into the family room and continue to play nicely. If the child is still stroppy, then close the door and let another 20 minutes pass. There's not much point in losing your temper because this shows great weakness and your partner must be on the same page as you. If children detect that they can get sympathy from one parent over the decisions of the other, they will take advantage. That must not happen. Even if you feel guilty about being out all day at work, you can't help the family situation by being soft and undermining your partner.

Cuddles and Affirmation

Kids need to feel loved. They need to know that even if they don't have the same abilities as the other kids in the family, they are still loved for their own individual characteristics. That's not a hard task for a parent. The best time to re-affirm this kind of love is when you take the time to put the kids to bed. Double up on your habits again. Trust the kids to wash and clean their teeth and then, when they are ready for bed, make it a family time. You will have happier kids and you will be happier as parents. This is a time of night when you can sing quiet songs together with the guitar, or read stories together.

When you deal with bedtime in this manner, you tend to have less fuss, but when the bedtime story or entertainment is over, draw boundaries. The kids do not leave their rooms after this time and the lights are put out. If a child needs a nightlight, then there are plug in night lights that add a little glow to the room and help the child to see the outlines of all of the room so that the child is not afraid.

Does Smacking Work?

There are laws in place that prohibit parents from being physical with their kids. A small tap on the hand if the child does something wrong doesn't hurt. I tend to reserve this for times when there is an urgent need. For instance, when I caught my daughter trying to put the dog in a full bath of water in which it would have drowned, I grabbed the dog and tapped her hand to let her know that what she was doing was very wrong.

You should never physically hurt a child and apart of physical harm, you can also cause harm to a child by shouting. Even if you are tired from your day's work, don't resort to shouting. What you demonstrate to a child when you shout is that this kind of behavior is acceptable. This is the kind of behavior that bullies use. Try to think of your home as being a safe place for your child and one that makes the child feel safe and loved. It is far better to talk to a child once the child has calmed down from the activity than it is to show anger by shouting.

TV, Internet and Cell Phones

Although you may be encouraged sometimes to deprive a child of something, you need to make your rules clear and universal for all of your children. If something is going to be taken away, they need to know the reason. If you believe that your child needs quiet time to reflect over being naughty, then the last thing you want is for them to be able to call their friends. Take the phone away and explain that the child can have it back when the child's behavior merits it.

In this day and age, it's very dangerous for kids to have Internet connection whenever they want it. Make sure that you have parent controls on your computer and that the children play suitable games for their ages. As far as TV goes, try to teach your children that TV is to be switched on when there is something worth watching and only after homework has been done. Stick to these rules and ask to look at the homework. A child who wants to watch something on TV is more inclined to do their homework if they know the TV will not be switched on until they have done what they need to do.

Chapter 8: How To Be A Positive Single Parent

When you first got married, you likely never thought you'd be using the phrase "single parent" to describe yourself. But divorce changes everything, and single parents have to work harder and smarter than married parents, particularly if your ex isn't heavily involved with your children. But by putting your children's needs first and ensuring you get the help you need, you can turn yourself into a positive model of single parenting and help your children escape your divorce unscathed.

Take Care of Yourself

You can't take care of your children if you don't take care of yourself. If you're having trouble coping with the anger and heartbreak of your divorce, it's time to consult with a professional who can help you navigate this new terrain. No parent can do it all, so don't feel guilty about taking a break from your kids. Enjoy your time alone when they're with your ex, and hire a babysitter or get help from a family member if you need a night off. You might feel like you're being selfish when you spend time away from your children, but your children need you to be emotionally healthy so that you can help them weather the storm of divorce.

Get Support

You've just lost one-half of your parenting team. It's unrealistic to think that you'll be able to do it alone; no single parent is fully alone. Your kids will need the love and affection of family and close friends to get through this time. Other adults can also serve as a sounding board for your child if she wants to talk about you or is worried that discussing the divorce with you will be upsetting. And if your ex isn't spending much time with your kids, other adults can help fill in the gap.

If at all possible, begin rallying the troops before you get divorced. But if you've already filed, don't be afraid to take people up on their offers to help. Try giving people specific tasks. Some of the things you can ask friends and family to do include:

Taking your kids on a fun outing once a week or once a month

Taking time to call and talk to your kids

Arranging sleepovers and play dates with your kids

Sharing their own experiences of divorce with your children

Picking your kids up from school or dropping them off at extracurricular activities when you're not able to

If your friends or family members have children, pool your resources. By helping your loved ones out, you'll avoid creating resentment and still be able to lean on a steady source of assistance.

Share Time with Your Children

Even if you've managed to keep it together for the first battle shots of divorce, odds are good that you are going to hate your ex for a few moments, a few weeks, or even a few years. When people go through nasty divorces, they often use their children to harm their exes, however; this will only harm your children. Courts give visitation to almost all parents, and trying to deny your ex time with your kids is a losing battle.

Study after study has shown that children are worse off after divorce when one parent is removed from the child's life. The only exception to this rule occurs if your ex is abusive. Although, remember that divorce distorts your perceptions. Don't make false allegations of abuse, and don't label merely annoying behavior — such as occasionally yelling or showing up late — as abusive. Even if your ex is abusive, your children will suffer if they don't spend time with him or her; supervised visitation may be a better option.

Look at your children's time with your ex as your chance to pursue your own interests and take a well-deserved break. Take up volunteering, get a new hobby, join a new sport, or try a class on something you've been curious about. Whatever it takes to get your mind off your divorce, do it.

Protect Your Children

Even if your ex is conspiring against you, your children should never know this. Above all else, they must be protected from adult concerns. Some basic rules to follow include:

Never talk negatively about your ex to your children.

Never tell your children to lie to your ex.

Don't say negative things about your ex's family or new romantic partner to your children.

Keep your telephone calls private; don't allow your kids to overhear fights with your ex.

If you're having legal or money problems, don't tell your kids, and more importantly, don't rely on them to solve these problems.

If you're feeling like an emotional wreck, get a baby-sitter or ask a loved one to help. When children see their parents in a moment of weakness, it can be frightening to them.

Limit Romance for a Little While

Sooner or later, you'll find someone who piques your interest; however, new relationships can be very stressful on your kids. It's best to keep your romances to yourself until you're sure this will be a long-term relationship. Children suffer when there's a never-ending stream of adults entering and exiting their lives. It's also unfair and unsafe to expose your children to someone you don't fully know.

Chapter 9: Learning The Skills Of Parenting

Parents unite! Complex as it is, it is possible to rear children into responsible, happy and welladjusted adults. From our end as parents, it will take patience and commitment. However, it will also take wisdom and experience. This is where our support system and access to those who know will play a big role.

No doubt parenting has its priceless rewards. No treasure could equal having our own flesh and blood continue the family line and seeing facets of ourselves in sons and daughters. We all look forward to seeing our grandchildren around us during visits and warm family gatherings. Grandchildren (well supported and taken cared of by their parents of course) are the rewards of old age.

It is a fact though, that being a parent is stressful and demanding. We are faced with situations that would require

Solomon's wisdom. Unfortunately, as most of us know, we are no Solomon. We face a thousand and one issues everyday.

For most of us who have been in this parenting business for more than 10 years, we found out that just when we knew all the answers, they changed all the questions! The issues differ from pregnancy to babies, from babies to toddlers, from toddlers to pre-schoolers. These go on and on until our precious children reach adulthood and have families of their own.

This might sound scary to first timers. However, we must remember that for every stressful situation, they are magical moments and lots of them. We just have to learn to appreciate them when they come and not be bogged down with the challenges of the day. Children, trying as they are most of the time, are a great source of joy.

When these situations and issues come though, don't we just wish that there is someone who could give us advice? We seek out that special parent who has gone through the same ordeal we are now in yet came out triumphant. How we wish we had a support group to discuss certain "case studies" so much like our own and find a list of solutions and alternatives. Then we could go back to our parenting with renewed confidence and hope instead of feeling hopeless and distraught.

Being parents, being good parents is challenging. No, it's not just challenging. It's tough! It is more than just providing for the material needs of our children. We'd like to be there for them, raise them to be winners or at least equip them with what they need to make a go at life.

On top of being parents, we are also faced with the challenges of our own careers, our relationships and our dreams. We have inner conflicts that we have to deal with. We have seemingly mundane tasks that are a necessary part of life. Don't we just wish we could find out how other parents cope? Just maybe, they have strategies to share with us or us with them. We all have our unique experiences that when shared could enrich each other.

It's really all about sharing what we know, what we have gone through, what works and what may not work. It's all about us and our children. It's all about being parents and what we could do to make each other better parents. Parenting is actually one long roller coaster ride for a lot of us. We could either be alone and agonize all through out the ride or with the help of others, enjoy it to the fullest.

How To Fail As A Parent

Anyone who has kids is immediately besought by many questions, and the weight of responsibility may lie heavily upon your shoulders. The fact is, there are many, many ways to fail when it comes to parenting, but the good news is that there are also many ways to succeed. The definition of failure as a parent will depend on many factors, including your culture, your hopes for your children, and the circumstances you find yourself in. In other words, one parent's successes, such as Donald Trump having both his children incorporated into his business and television show, may seem to another parent to have been failures, the failure of a parent to spend enough time with and thinking about his offspring. Failing as a parent, therefore, will be dependent on your goals. There are still areas in which it is easy for us all to fail as parents, no matter what our goals for our children may be.

The first way many parents fail is by putting their children ahead of themselves, especially during their very early years. More and more research is showing that the most important time in a child's life, in terms of development, are the preschool ages, including infancy. Your child needs you around at this stage, mothers and fathers both. It can seem impossible with the pressures and responsibilities of work to make the time necessary for the kids, but it is an important consideration nonetheless. This may be a time when you have to let some of those promotions pass for a time in order to serve the best interests of your family.

Another big mistake many parents make is either expecting too much or too little of their children, at any age, logically speaking. This applies to parents of teenagers as well as babiesthe human brain is still developing right into the twenties, and even teenagers will not think of matters in the same logical way as adults. On the other hand, you do not want to underestimate your offspring's powers of perception- as with many issues in parenting, there is a very fine line to walk, and you must base it on your knowledge of your child.

This brings us to the final area that will bring about failure when it comes to raising your children- by listening to everybody else. It seems that these days, everyone has an opinion as to how your children should be raised. There is a lot of conflicting advice, and lots that will just not work when it comes to your own children. Again, you know your children best and the final decision in matters will be up to you; base your decision on what has worked on the past. If this approach does not work, then it is time to try the alternatives suggested by someone else (and start with someone with a proven track record with their own children!) Again, this is a fine linedo not ignore your doctor's advice when it comes to medical needs.

Chapter 10: Inability For Undivided Attention

With the exception of death, single parenting is a choice that is decided by the parents —whether it is one parenting selfishly making a personal choice, or both parents deciding to terminate the relationship, the choice is theirs.Children are put in the middle of these decisions and forced to live with them and the outcome that comes with that decision.However the parent decides to conduct their life, their choices and actions directly affect their children.Parents are more equipped to adjust to the changing dynamics of terminating relationships, moving and realigning their lives to fit their new situation.Unfortunately, however, children, kids and teens are not that well-equipped emotionally to adapt to those changes.

Unfortunately, we cannot change the ever growing population of single parenting.Statistically, single parent households will exceed dual parent households within the next twenty years.And although we may not be able to alter the course of people's lives, we can however be better informed of the perils of single parenting.Perhaps if people closely looked at the affects and reasons why single parenting is a bad idea, they would rethink their decisions.

Single parenting has a laundry list of negative affects on children, kids and teens.Those effects range from issues in the classroom and relating to other students or authority all the way to emotional disorders like social issues and behavioral issues.And there are many reasons why those factor struggles present themselves to the kids.

A good example is when a single parent is experiencing a problem or an issue, the child is also experiencing that same problem or issue, albeit more indirectly, however, nevertheless, the children are still put in a situation where the parent's problems become their problems. When the child sees the struggling, no matter how hard the parent is trying to cope, the child will recognize there is a problem and feelings of anxiousness and fear begin to manifest themselves within the child.

Children and young people are being forced to partake in the adult world far before their time and most of these young people are still developing themselves. There are in the process of learning how to survive in their own world, with their own set of problems when they are forced to take on the burden of carrying their parent's struggle. And although no parent wants this for their child or is asking for that they embrace their struggle as their own, it is a force that cannot be helped.

In addition to this very real scenario, when parents experience a crisis in their lives, there is an inability to not allow it to consume them, and when that happens, they are less likely to meet the needs of their children. The emotional juggle of different circumstances, problems and pressing issues is overwhelming, and of course two parent households have pressures and crises as well. However, the difference is they can relinquish emotional burdens on each other and that allows them to have the ability to meet their kid's needs, when they need to be met.

Chapter 11

There are strategies that sort of force and mold behavior. Patterns of action seems to be the key. But there are a couple of ways this happens, lovingly executed or achieved through angry punishment.

Here's the problem. Any grandparent can tell there's an evolution, a change in attitude. About every 10 years or so, they may gauge transformation and make an assessment. What they surmise is that there is an obvious growing level of contempt for authority.

You read it and see it on the television news. Recently, a contemptuous young adult took her parents to court. No wonder seniors attribute children's attitudes to what can best be described as a child-centered culture that puts children in charge instead of parents.

One news commentator put it this way, "If children don't learn that society has rules of conduct and consequences for bad behavior, they grow up into a culture in which they're often useless. They can't work, they can't get a job, and they have no respect for people above them."

Personally, I can't agree more. But just how can this model be achieved? What is the best way, through human discipline reasoning, learning by example, or behavior due to fear of consequence?

Parents use spanking generally in order to reduce undesirable conduct and increase appropriate behavior. A very important factor in exercising this practice is to say what you mean and mean what you say. But leadership becomes compromised, because threats are not enforced. That emboldens undesirable performance. The results cannot possibly meet the first parenting goal. So that does nothing but cause frustration.

Researchers have looked at effects on at least three objectionable behaviors in children who are spanked: non-compliance in the short term, non-compliance in the long term, and aggression.But this area is hard to study in the home because spanking rarely occurs at all nor in front of strangers. It's not even possible to study in the laboratory because of the prohibition against hurting subjects.

It is again time to reflect a bit on this thought. Why, when it comes to child psychology, is everything measured clinically and scientifically? My personal experience in this matter is worth mentioning. My wife, mother of two boys, almost four years apart, rarely used corporal punishment to adjust behavior. I emphasize rare, because on a few occasions, as toddlers, this punishment was executed. On several instances, people voluntarily commented, in public, what perfect angels they were. "How did you manage to raise such perfect little gentlemen?"

The trick, if you want to call it that, was simple. She meant what she said and said what she meant. Maybe she inherited a unique stare which was best described as a "look" from her mother. I've heard a lot about "the-look" and it is very intimidating.

The LOOK was psychologically attached to a belt. That's what made it scary. Her mother used it many times. It didn't take long to do what was essentially necessary to avoid "the-look".

The point made is the fact that children learn consequences only when there's legitimacy to threats. It doesn't matter what the so called experts say, if there's ever a line to cross that automatically triggers a resistance. The perpetrator understands the consequences, and so non-compliant behavior most likely will not happen. This is the strength of real domestic leadership.

When three year old Tommy drew all over the bedroom wall with crayons, there was a line crossed. He didn't get spanked, but suffered the consequences. His mother taught him how to clean the art work off the wall. Funny thing about that incident was his remark, "Isn't this fun mom?" Never again was wall art discovered though.

They didn't grow up with a whole lot of toys. The boys learned that when mother draws a line, she means what she says. "Pick up all your toys and put them away. Any toys laying around tonight goes to Goodwill."

All right, you've heard it but disagree that Fear-Based Behavior works. You say that's Pollyannaish. Experts will continue to adamantly claim that it is much more effective and easier to change a behavior when you have positive reasons rather than negative reactions.

Sure, when it comes to mature minds, this makes perfect sense. A misbehaved two or three year old, on the other hand, does not respond to optimistic perceptions, but certainly understands a slap to the hand or rear.

Meanwhile, a distinguished list of experts denounce spanking as ineffective, even dangerous. They all claim corporal punishment teaches a child to fear his parents, not to respect them. Forced behavior, as they report, can injure a child and warp his understanding of how to interact with others.

Well now, according to their experiments, **lab-rats** determine that it's okay to attack someone to get their own way. Good grief - experts also warn that children who have this antisocial lesson beaten into them are more likely to exhibit violent behavior later in life.

Chapter 12: Discipline Positively

Positive discipline is not only about teaching good behaviors and reinforcing them. It is also about maintaining a good positive relationship with your child. Emphasis is placed on lovingly reprimanding the child. Understand what the child is going through and what he is trying to say. Parents should know and understand the child's developmental abilities. They should be more sensitive to what the child needs, and if they are being satisfactorily met. The problem may not really lie on the child's behavior, but on the relationship they have with their parents. When dealing with the child, maintain respect and use empathy. Be sensitive to the child's emotions. Parents should carefully study the circumstances of the behavior, before imposing their own will. When doing so, make the requests in an affirmative manner. Avoid frequent use of negative words like "Don't do this" and "Don't do that".

When kids behave badly and hurt others, parents often force them to apologize. Learn to let the child express his emotions and help him work out his next course of action. Help him to realize the consequences of his actions. Avoid putting labels on his behavior, such as him being a "bad kid". If the child is hurt, tend to him first. Avoid giving harsh logical consequences.

Here are a few steps to positively discipline your kids.

1. Encourage your child

Discipline need not leave a child feel bad about themselves. Parents should be able to build up their child's self-esteem. Parents need to focus on 3 things in order to encourage their child.

a. Internal evaluation

Parents should more focus on what the child is going through. Let them be aware that what they feel matters more than what the parents feel about them. Help raise their self-esteem by focusing more on how they see and feel about themselves.

b.Contributions

Show appreciation on how they contributed to family dynamics. Put more emphasis on how helpful they were, how they made the whole situation better. Avoid giving judgments on what they did. Appreciate the results as they are.

c.Effort and Improvement

Appreciate the child's efforts on good behavior. Give attention on how they have improved their actions. Avoid focusing on whether they were successful or not. Praising them for winning might send a message that winning is the only appreciative act they can have. Encourage them on the efforts and improvements they made. Congratulating them on their awards is only secondary. This way, they feel that winning is not the most important thing.

2.Be a role model

The best way to make children behave a certain way is to model the desired behavior. Children, especially preschool and school-aged ones, look for role models. They follow what behaviors they see. Parents should be the first ones to follow the established rules. Walk the talk.

3.Set limits

Limits are actually acceptable for children. It makes them feel safe and secure. However, expect them to test these limits often. Be firm. The limits you set should always be followed. Everyone should follow, for more effective disciplinary measures. If children see that not everyone follows and gets away with it, they will likely disobey as well.

4.Learn to Ignore

Ignoring certain behaviors may not suit well for parents who are keen on making their children behave. Yelling and hitting your child is still attention. Children may become desperate for your attention that they opt to have negative type of attention than none at all. In reality, you are actually reinforcing negative behavior by your yelling. Ignoring the behavior could work, by sending a message that such misdeeds do not warrant any of your attention. Ignoring includes no eye contact, not talking or responding to the child until after the negative behavior ends. Example is when a child asks for something in a whining voice. Ignore the whining instead of yelling for the child to stop. This way, the child will come to realize that whining will not get him what he wants.

There are instances that ignoring is not warranted. A sure indication that ignoring is not advisable is when the child is hurting himself, others or damaging property. You need to intervene as safety is compromised.

In order for this strategy to be effective, follow these guidelines:

a. Do not give any recognition to the undesirable behavior.

Avoid any form of attention while the child exhibits the unacceptable behavior. Do not even attempt to argue. It will be futile.

b. Consistency

Always be consistent. It sends a definite message that the behavior will always be unacceptable. If you oscillate between ignoring and recognizing, the child will think that he needs to increase the intensity of the negative behavior in order to get the desired attention.

c. Give attention to the child as soon as the behavior stops.

After the child stops acting unacceptably, show that you still care for the child. Be able to show that you were ignoring him because of the unacceptable behavior, not because you no longer care for him. Reassure him of your love and care.

5. Establish rules

Rules are needed for predictability, stability, and consistency. It is good to include older children when setting up rules to make them feel included and important. Goal setting that involves the children makes them feel more responsible and feel better about themselves. Chances are, children who were part of setting up the rules are more likely to follow them.

Chapter 13: Discipline In A Positive Way

Discipline is a way of behaving in a specific manner. Everyone behaves in a certain way and follow a set of rules. From childhood we are taught to eat, talk, walk, and behave in a certain manner. However, it is important to pass on these set of rules to our children in a positive way.

There are two ways we can handle our children. Either we do it negatively (scold, spank, and frighten) or positively (communicate, understand, and help). We need to understand that most toddlers cannot distinguish between good and bad. We have to keep our cool and handle them wisely. As a parent it is our responsibility to make them understand. We cannot just give them instructions and expect them to obey. There are various ways we can deal with our little ones in a positive way. Appreciation is one thing you can use. When a child does something good, praise them. It is important that they realize they have done something right and feel good about it.

Many children cry when they see someone else handling something which belongs to them. For example if a child sees some other kid playing with his toy, he may cry or hit the other kid. Teach your child to share things. You may share with them something that they like and set an example. It is also important not to give in to all that a child asks for. There are times when we may have to put our foot down. Rewarding the child is another way of getting things done. When a child misbehaves instead of scolding them try to analyze the reason. They may be upset, frustrated, hurt etc. Be there for your children. It is alright to become a child with your child. Show them how to do things that they are finding difficult. If a child does something wrong let them know about it. Toddlers will explore things. Don't force the child to do something. Observe what they enjoy and as long as it is safe and right, let them do it. Let them do things independently. Let them know that it is alright to make mistakes but make sure you show them the correct way of doing it. There may be times they will make a mess, spoil and even break things. But we need to remember most of the time; they don't intend to do it as they are learning.

Many times we tend to ignore a child's fear. If your child is scared of something, try to understand and talk through it. Do not ignore it. If your child is scared to sleep alone in the dark for example use a lamp. Also avoid developing any fear in your child. E.g. Your child doesn't listen to you and you lock them in a dark room telling them a monster will come and take them away. Instead tell them they will be rewarded if they listen to you. And keep your promise. It is necessary to discipline your child in a right and positive way or else they run higher risk of turning out to be aggressive, violent, stressed and anxious later in life.

Surviving The Terrible Twos

Terrible twos is stage where children become cranky, they throw tantrums and they are difficult to please. This is just a passing phase. There are so many stories about terrible twos that it is actually considered as a very dreaded stage for many. I have heard all kinds of crazy things including people saying terrible twos are God's way of ensuring we don't have any more children, which of course is a bit silly if you ask me.

There is no easy way to handle the terrible twos but there are ways to handle these situations. While in this phase children start throwing tantrums. They scream and make mess around in the house. They are fussy when things don't happen their way. They will do opposite of what you ask them to. At this stage they are curious and indecisive. They are inquisitive. They try to be independent. They have no control on their feelings, but there is no real way to get away from this completely.

We just need to find ways to get through the terrible twos and ease out this early childhood period of time.

It is important to set rules. Make sure the rules are set and they are clear. Go through the rules with your children. Let your children know about them. Let them know if the rules are broken they will have to face the consequences. It is most likely possible that the toddler is trying to express something which we do not understand.

Speak to them and try to understand what they are trying to express. For example, there will be times they may want to eat on their own. Let them be on their own even if they are spilling little food, this will allow them to experience just one more thing they are curious about, they find themselves in a completely new and cool world where they are starting to realize the endless possibilities found in it. We should appreciate them as they are trying something new, and instead of making it seem like a bad thing, we should enjoy this time with our children for it will be the only time you will ever see them this way.

Don't give in to your child's demands every time regardless of wherever you are. Be firm and let them realize that you won't give in to their demands. Talk to your children. Ask them what exactly they want. Discuss things with them. Sometimes they throw tantrums just to seek your attention. Spend time with them. If they want to make their own decisions give them choices.

When they throw a tantrum it can help to express your displeasure. You don't need to shout at them or spank them. However, let them know you are not happy about their behaviors. Do not lose control. Praise them when they listen to you. If they learn something new reward them and make sure to always keep them busy as this will satisfy their urge to express their curiosity and exploration while at the same time burning some of the extra energy they have.

Even in public do not get embarrassed. Everyone knows about this phase of the terrible twos. Hence most people will not be surprised. If your child stays in a play group and spends time with the caregiver, make sure you let the caregiver know about his habits. You don't have to be so strict, though, throughout this phase of the terrible twos you will face a new challenge every day. Just stay calm and don't try to get away from that situation completely but learn a few new things as you will find in this book that will help to make it easier for you and your child.

Terrible twos is just a phase and it does not prove that you are not a good parent as some first time parents might tend to believe. This is just a normal development stage. If you help your child through this phase of the terrible twos you will be building the right foundation for mutual understanding that will carry on throughout their lives.

Chapter 14: Benefits Of Being A Single Parent

Single parents are found in every society in the world today. This implies that there are many broken families that are formed due to one reason or another.

However, many nations are mindful of the difficulties and struggles a parent goes through and put in as many benefits to assist the parent.

A parent will have at least one child to care for and that will be a long and heavy investment. You can check out if you, as a parent, qualify for the federal benefits.

Eligibility of Single Parent Benefits

Firstly, age matters. A parent can be of any age. A parent below the age of 16 to 19, in full time studies or intending to be employed in that same age bracket is eligible to federal assistance in terms of financial aid.

There are many charitable organizations, corporations and support groups for parents that offer much more besides financial aid.

Emotional Support

A parent cannot cope with all the emotions that may swell up in various caring situations; hence, a support group is crucial to maintain the mental and emotional health of a parent.

Regular meet ups with such support groups prove to be a great benefit to parents who need to learn how to care for their children while juggling between jobs and family. The role of a parent is quite demanding to function as a father and mother.

You may find loads of information on techniques and ways to care for your children as a parent, but none is as effective as meeting with other parents and professional counselors who can share from live experiences.

Free School Program

Parents can benefit from a federal incentive for parents where their children can get schooling benefits such as free tuition, food and study materials. This would ease the burden of parents, especially if there is more than one child in the family.

Health Benefits

There are certain health benefits for parents that qualify you for free medication or medical check-ups for yourself and your children if you are a parent. There may be some visits from the local child or family services department to check on your state of livelihood. Some states include free or discounted dental treatments, glasses and vision tests or travel options.

Community Benefits

There may be community care and share programs for parents where free activities are offered to parents and their children such as public library access and membership, plays and local activities. Assistance of sorts may be offered free of charge for parent families.

Chapter 15: Following Through On Promises

On the heels of consistency is follow-through. No, we're not talking about swinging bat. Follow-through means that you do what you say you will do; good or bad.

From a Bill Cosby comedy routine...

Bill Cosby: [after spanking the kids] My wife comes downstairs with a broken stick. She throws it on the table and begins to talk out loud to... NOBODY! "Gonna tell me that you're not going to do something when I tell you to do something. I mean you MOVE when I say move! Think I carried you in my body for nine months so you can roll your eyes at me? I'll roll that little head of yours down on the floor. You don't know who you're fooling with. I'll beat you until you can't grow anymore!"

Now, as many laughs as Mr. Cosby got for his routine, we are left with the assurance that his wife was not going to beat anyone. We all see ourselves in his portrayal of frustration and hollow threats. Every parent has found himself confronted with a child's act that is so over the line that he is left sputtering with indignity.

Children also have a sense of humor. They love attention and will go to great lengths to get it. Leaving a parent sputtering is just the kind of attention they love most. As long as the parent is spouting ridiculous threats, the child knows he or she is safe. No follow through.

Obviously the point here is not comic punishment threats, but the suggestion that when confronted with the unexpected, take a few moments to calmly assess the situation and respond calmly and appropriately. That sort of consistent follow through is far more effective with the least amount of action. Just as "B" follows "A" a child should understand that each transgression carries with it a predictable punishment and they should simply expect it. That sort of attention holds no allure. That is what follow through is all about.

Punishment is not the only application of consistent promise. Do you find yourself saying, "This weekend we'll go to a movie," and when the weekend comes, you never go near a theatre? Do we bargain with promises? Is this sort of bribery practiced to get good behavior or cooperation at a sticky time? We've all done it. When we don't follow through, our word loses potency and that same ambivalence is applied to all our parenting efforts. A child needs to feel confident in their parents' integrity. When you make a promise, keep your word. When the need for parental intervention occurs, keep your calm and respond with wisdom and the maturity the situation calls for. Avoid making empty promises.

Chapter 16: Getting Rid Of The Guilt

There are all kinds of things that a single father may find himself feeling guilty about. He may not be top notch when it comes to organizing the home and feel that his care of the kids is inadequate. Care of the children isn't measured by how neatly you iron the sheets, or how you remember to wash their gym gear ready for their next event. It's about remembering that the tooth fairy may need to visit a certain bedroom. It's about knowing what makes your kids happy and it's also about learning new skills.

People don't suddenly go from being in a marriage to single parenthood without feeling some kind of inadequacy. That applies to single women as well. While you may not feel that you can give the kids what a mother can, you can give them what you are and you should never be apologetic about that. What you are is their father. You are learning all about what it takes to be a single parent and you can't go through this if you weaken your position by always feeling inadequate and guilty because you didn't know something.

Even if you were in a marriage, you would still feel a certain amount of guilt perhaps for being at work too long and not seeing your kids growing up. You may not have the same organizational ability as your wife had, but what you do have is sufficient love to have decided that you want custody of the kids in the first place and that's far more valuable than all the organizational skills put together.

Learn with the kids and make it a fun exercise. If you can't be there because of work, don't just drop the kids off on babysitters. Make the situation something they can look forward to or can photograph so that you can share it when you are at home. That way, the kids always feel secure in the knowledge that dad's there for them, regardless of whether he can actually take the time off work. If you need to, invest in a digital camera for the kids and tell them you don't want to miss anything about their growing up. That makes them feel like your presence is always something they can feel secure about.

Discuss holidays and work out what you are going to do together. If you're a single parent, you may not have money to spare, but kids don't mind camping in the back garden. What matters more to them is that dad was there with them, enjoying the holiday. When the kids make demands of money for school outings and you find yourself short, try to think of ways that the whole family can economize so that they can go. Work with them, knowing in advance and perhaps between you, you can come up with ways to raise that extra cash. Don't feel guilty because you don't have it. Feel that every stumbling block in your family situation is an opportunity to find another way. Perhaps the kids can have a garage sale and get rid of old stuff they don't play with any more. Perhaps you have items that you can sacrifice toward those school extras. There's always a way and with optimism and imagination, a single father can make all of these things happen with a little planning.

Don't feel guilty if you have to work when the kids need you. Be part of it and make sure that you check in on them so they know you care. I remember my father couldn't be at a special event and I was very hurt by it until he did something extremely special that I will never forget. It was a choir event. I had to sing a solo and I wanted him to hear it. He handed me a hymn book with a leather cover and my name engraved on it saying the words "I can't be with you, but you will know I am there in spirit." I sang my solo and I didn't feel abandoned, as that book was in my hand and my father's sentiments went with me to my special event.

A single father has a very difficult balancing act to perform. You can do it, but do it in such a way that you create wonderful childhood memories for your kids, rather than regrets of dad always being negative and unavailable. Dads can be a wonderful influence on their kids and sometimes all it takes is a little thoughtfulness and a little planning. As kids, we had been through the uncertainty of divorce. We had been through the clash of personalities between mom and dad. We had been through all of the doubts and uncertainties that arise from custody arguments. At the end of it all, we came away from our childhoods with the kind of security that money can't buy, sure that our dad was the best influence in our lives, and always happy to go home to share life with him.

When you get past the regrets and the uncertainties of divorce, and can concentrate on the relationship between yourself and your kids in a very positive way, you create a family story all of your own. Make yourself the kind of father you would be proud to have and all the insecurity becomes something of the past. Your children appreciate you and you are the first person they come to when they need a friendly shoulder to cry on. That's all you can do as a parent and there's no guilt attached to that. You will watch your little boy turn into a man and your little girl turn into a woman but for now, you must enjoy them and let them enjoy you regardless of your circumstances. My dad did exactly that and we became the best of friends. That's when you know that you have given your kids the best that you can and have been the father that your kids deserved.

Chapter 17: How To Solve Problems That Arise

There are times when your teen is going to need your help. Whether you notice an issue early on or your teen comes to you to discuss an issue they have noticed, it is important to figure out the next steps to take to get the teen the help that they need. While there are a number of things that you can do, this is a trying time for any parent to go through with their children. Here are some of the best things that you can do in order to solve these issues when they arise and get the best results for your family.

Listen to Your Child

If your child is coming to you with the problems listed in this guidebook, it is important that you stop and listen to them. It was not easy for them to come to you with these issues. While you may feel that they are just for attention or because you didn't get one toy or another for them, it is still important to sit down and listen to what the child is saying.

You know your child. You know when they are doing something for attention or when they are actually worried about a problem and reaching out to you for help. Don't go through denial and assume that an honest confession of addiction or thoughts of suicide is just a plea for attention. If they are being honest, it was really hard for them to come out to you and they are hoping that you will be able to help them.

When your child comes to talk to you about these issues, set aside time for them. Turn off the other distractions and really listen to what they have to say. This may seem like a silly thing, but with so much going on in life, it is easy to get distracted and not really hear what is being said. Allow your child to talk through the issue with you and give your opinion, advice, and support as much as possible. The only way that you can really help your child is to hear what they are telling you.

Get Them Help

The first thing that you should do after your child announces that they have an issue, or you find out in some other way, is to get them the help that they deserve. This can be a hard thing for some parents to do. You have just found out that your child is doing something that breaks your heart. No parent wants to hear that their child is depressed and not feeling good. They don't want to hear that their child wants to commit suicide or is dealing with addiction. They want their child to be happy and healthy for years to come.

But despite what you are feeling at the time, it is important to concentrate all your efforts on your child. They are the ones who are going through this tough period and they need someone who is going to be right there with them through it all. Whether you are having a hard time or not, it is important to get your child some help.

There are a variety of places you can turn to provide help for your child. Treatment centers for addictions are the best places to start if your child is dealing with something like this. A psychologist is good for those dealing with depression and thoughts of suicide. You may need to call around a little bit to figure out who is going to work the best for your situation. Getting into treatment is the first step for recovery, but finding the right help and not having to worry about costs or picking the wrong one can weigh heavily on the minds of many parents.

In addition, you should consider some counseling for yourself. Many parents forget that they need some attention to. You are going through all those hard emotions that were discussed above and dealing with this while still providing the support that your child needs is not always easy. Consider seeking some counseling for yourself and your spouse during this time. Not only can it help you to feel a bit better about this process, and understand that this is not your fault, but it sets you up so you are better able to take care of your child while they go through the difficult process as well.

As soon as you find out there is some issue going on with your child, it is time to step up and find the right treatment that is going to make this better. The sooner you are able to find the treatment, the better so that the child does not go forward with any of the thoughts and the addiction doesn't get worse. Treatment is hard and no one is going to like it, but it is a necessary part of the process needed to get through these tough times.

Show Support

Being supportive is your main goal in this whole process. It does not matter how you personally feel about the situation, you can deal with that in therapy if you need. What does matter is how you react to your child and the situation. Those teens who got into trouble with depression, suicidal thoughts, and addiction and who had some support right from the beginning were much more likely to get through the whole process and not relapse.

Think about it; how likely were you to finish up with a treatment or make a change when you thought no one cared? If you thought that it didn't matter whether you got the help that you needed or just kept on the same path, you were not going to make a change. It is easier to keep on the same course rather than making a change. But when you have a group of people supporting you through it all, it is much easier to see that change is the way to go and not relapse back as you go.

Don't be Judgmental

This is not the time for judgment. Yes, your child did something that is not good and is having bad thoughts or stuck with an addiction. And perhaps at some point you had warned them against using drugs, hanging out with that group of friends, or some other thing that may have prevented the issue from the start. But that does not matter right now. Your teen does not need a lecture at this time about how bad they are. They either know that they did something wrong or they don't want to hear about it, and sitting there with a lot of judgement is going to make the situation worse.

Come at this whole process from a point of understanding. While your child did something that is horrible or is having bad thoughts, they are not bad people. They made mistakes or perhaps something happened along the way to make them feel helpless. They are doing the best that they can in this situation. Sometimes it is hard to remember that they are children still, not adults, and sometimes the actions don't always match up how we would like. But when you reserve the judgement and instead focus on the treatment and how good your teen really is, you are going to see some great results.

Encourage Their Progress

Be encouraging throughout this process. While this may seem like a challenge, you need to be there encouraging your child as much as possible. This is not an easy process for them. Whether you noticed there was a problem first or they came to you does not matter. You need to be there for them and encourage even the smallest steps forward. If they admitted they had a problem, be encouraging and supportive of that. If they made it five days addiction free, make it a little celebration.

The more that you are able to celebrate the little milestones, the better off you are going to be. This can help your teenager to feel good about the situation and they are going to feel more encouraged for continuing on. When the teen feels like things aren't going their way or that no one cares about whether they improve or not, they have no reason to continue. But if they see that you are celebrating even the smallest of accomplishments, you are going to see that they improve so much faster than on their own.

Watch Out for Signs of Regression

Treatment and your support are going to do a ton when it comes to helping your teen get through these hard times. But, they aren't always full proof. Regression can often happen during the treatment, or shortly after the treatment is through. If you aren't watching for these signs, the teen could spiral back to the behaviors that they did in the past, and it is going to be much harder to deal with the second or third time around.

Learn what some of the signs of trouble are will make this process a bit easier. If you didn't learn these from the first time around, make sure to learn them now. It would be a shame to have something happen to a loved one because you were not able to help them in the way that they needed. If you notice that there are some signs of regression going on, take note and talk to their doctor or psychologist from before to see what the next steps will be and if the child would benefit from going through the treatment again.

Be Available to Help

During this whole time, you should make yourself available to help as much as possible. This can be hard to handle sometimes, but if your teen feels like they are alone, the thoughts and feelings are going to start causing issues again. Rather than letting this happen, you should be available to help as much as possible so you can see some success.

There are a number of ways that you can be available to help out through this whole process. Offer to take them to the treatments, help out with any of the "homework" they may get, be available to talk anytime they are feeling bad and need a friend. Each situation is going to be a bit different and you will need to provide help and support in different ways. Often, just being there for your teen as they go through this trying time can be enough to help make things a bit better.

Keep Them in Treatment Plan

Throughout this process, your teen may feel like they no longer want to be in the treatment plan. They may not think they have a problem, not like the fact that their friends or classmates are making fun of them for being in the treatment plan, or think that it is just too hard to get through the whole thing. But until they are done with the whole treatment plan, they are not going to be able to be fully healed of the issue at hand.

Many teenagers will get out of treatment early, before they are ready, and then find that it is not the answer that they needed. The thoughts are still there, haunting them and making them feel bad. If your teen stops the treatment plan before they are ready, they are just going to revert back to their old ways of acting and thinking. Before taking your teen out of a treatment plan, whichever one you chose, make sure to talk to their doctor or psychologist to figure out if this is the right plan or whether they need just a little more time. It may be tough, but a few extra weeks or so in the treatment could mean the difference when it comes to saving the life of your child.

Don't Belittle Their Issue

During this process, you should never belittle your teen. This is not the time to show your emotions and frustration at the process; doing so is just going to put you far behind in the whole healing process. When you belittle them, asking things like how would they fall into drugs or how they could be so stupid, will just make them withdraw and you will no longer be able to help them. Yes, this is going to be a trying time for you as well and you may not understand how things got so out of control. But at this point you need to be lifting your teen up and ignoring all the negative feelings in your mind.

This is not going to be easy. Consider getting some help for yourself as well. You are also going through a tough time with your teenager whether they are suffering from suicidal thoughts, depression, or addiction. You may need to talk some of this out and have someone on your side helping you through this tough time so you can have control over the emotions and not ruin your teens chances of getting better because of the hard time that you are going through as well. Don't assume you are going to be fine, get some help so that you are able to be there for your teen through these hard times.

Show Understanding Through Tough Times

There are times that are going to be tougher for your teen compared to others. They may be going through a detox from their addiction. They could suffer from suicidal thoughts and need help getting these to turn around. The treatment plan is not the only thing that is going to be tough; their friends and others who know them may start acting differently around your teenager after they find out about the problem. This can make the situation even harder on your teenager and there are going to be times when they feel upset, angry, and ready to give up.

During this time, you need to show that you understand how difficult the whole process is for them. Showing some empathy shows that you really care about the situation and that you want to be there to help. Let them be angry, let them do a little shouting and show that the situation is not fair. This emotion is a part of the whole process and when they go through it, they are not angry at you, but more showing some of their mixed up emotions as they are getting back together.

Learning how to solve some of the problems that are going to arise with your child is not always easy. There are going to be some trying times for your child and they may not know how to get through it all. But when you withhold the judgment and learn how to help them with a proper treatment plan, understanding, and providing them with the support that they need, it becomes easier to give your teen the help them need to get back on the right track and back to their normal selves in no time.

Chapter 18: Tips You Can Use

It is important to have tips at hand to ensure that you are using the best techniques possible while you are disciplining your child, and to help ensure you are changing your behavior, if needed, as well as theirs.

1.Understand what your child can do and what your child cannot do. Remember that all children are different and they develop at a different rate. What you may think of as rebellion or your child refusing to do what you ask, may simply be that your child does not know how to do what you are asking or is incapable of doing it.

2.Always think before you speak. Before you make a rule, make sure that you are going to be able to stick to it. Before you set out a consequence, make sure that you are going to be able to stick to it as well. Before you ever make a promise to your child, be sure that you are going to be able to keep it. You also need to think about what you are asking of your child; make sure that it is realistic. Finally, think before saying no. Is there really any reason for you to say no, or are you just speaking before thinking?

3. Never give in. Children throw tantrums so that they can get what they want. When you give in to this behavior you are reinforcing it. Instead, refuse to give in, refuse to encourage bad behavior and teach your child that this is not the way for him to get what he wants.

4. Be consistent. Make sure that your rules do not change from day to day. It is important for the child to know what is expected of him each day and for this to remain the same. If you are frequently changing what you expect out of your child, it will only confuse him and it will encourage them to push the limits. Children will naturally push the limits to find out how far they can go and what the limits are; if the expectations keep

changing so do the limits, and this will leave the child feeling confused.

5. Make sure you pay attention to the way the child is feeling. Emotions cause behaviors; if you find that your child misbehaves when he is emotional, or when certain events take place, you need to address the way that he is feeling. Explain to the child that you understand he is upset, but he is still expected to follow the rules.

6. Learn from your mistakes and let your child see you doing so. If you yelled at your child or overreacted, learn from the situation and your mistake, express to the child that you are sorry for what happened, and then make sure that it does not happen again. Make sure that you are providing your child with a role model that knows how to accept mistakes and learn from them.

7. Take the time to understand the reason behind the behavior. It is your job as the parent to find out why the child is

behaving in the manner that he or she is behaving. Children can only do what they know; this means that if they do not know how to behave well, or have never been taught to behave better, they cannot be expected to do so. You have to teach them what you want them to know and do.

Ask yourself if your child is behaving the way he is because he is looking for attention from you. This is one of the main reasons that a child misbehaves, and oftentimes simply getting off the phone or taking time away from Facebook will allow you to give the child the attention that he or she needs.

8.Focus on controlling yourself and not controlling the child. Children mimic our behavior; instead of focusing on what the child is doing, spend some time focusing on what you are doing. If, for example, you spend a lot of time yelling or throwing things, you cannot expect your child to behave differently until you do. Teach your child to handle his anger and frustration by being the example that he needs. Learn how to handle your own anger and frustration and your child will learn from your actions.

9.Give more attention to the good behavior in order to get rid of the bad behavior. If the child is misbehaving because he thinks it is the only way for him to get the attention he desires, focus on giving him that attention when he behaves well. Oftentimes, children will misbehave simply to get attention. To a child any attention is better than no attention, and if he is not getting attention for the good things that he does he will misbehave to get it. Reward him when he does good. Tell him he has done a good job and that you are proud of him.

10. Redirect him when you see the signs of impending misbehavior. Instead of saying no over and over, redirect the child, taking his attention away from what is bothering him, and give him time to cool down. One example of this is a child who misbehaves

in the grocery store; he could be redirected to help put food in the cart or hold the list or coupons. Simply keeping him busy, making him feel that he is helping, and getting his mind off of what he was doing will get rid of the unwanted behavior.

By learning some simple tips, you can make a huge difference when it comes to the way your child behaves. Choose a few tips to start out with and make small changes – you will see an amazing outcome.

Chapter 19: Keeping Some Normalcy For The Children After A Divorce

Both the children and the parent need stability after a divorce. Try to limit as many changes as you can due to the divorce so that your children can hold on to as much normalcy as possible. This prevents the children from feeling as if they are being up rooted from part of their family and losing their family structure at the same time. If possible try to keep the children in the same school; if you are forced to move then try to remain within the same district particularly until the end of the school year.The children are having a hard enough time dealing with the divorce so they should not have to deal with the emotions of making new friends.

Children get attached to family and friends from both sides so it can get tricky to continue those relationships. Talk openly with family and friends to find out where everyone is at with the rituals that were conducted as a married couple because you don't want anyone to feel out of place. If everyone is okay with the family rituals then they should continue, even through there will be a void with only one of the spouses present. If you ex-spouse has a ritual with the children then they should continue to do so. The children will most likely look forward to that time with the parent. There are still memories to be made for the children and they should be allowed. Ask them about new traditions they may want to incorporate into their lives. The more habits and routines you can preserve from your old way of life, the more stable and secure the children will be in their new life.

Establish Clear Rules for Children Of Divorced Parents

After a divorce it is important to provide, order, rules, routine and a firm foundation amidst uncertainty; however, it can very difficult to establish clear rules that both parents agree on when they don't live in the same home. Each household cannot have two different sets of rules because the children will use them to their advantage in many situations.It's a fact that parents are going to have different opinions on the rules associated with each individual household. You should do you best to compromise on those things that you feel are the most important and make a list for future reference.

It's much easier for the children to adjust if they have a set routine as they move from one home to the next.The parents should have a well defined curfew for the children to adhere to because it prevents the children from wanting to spend the most time with the parent that allows them the most freedom. Regardless of the rules they should never be permanently set in stone and should be evaluated and modified when needed. If both ex-spouses are able to communicate well then they should have no problem discussing any issues with the children and modifying the schedule. This type of action portrays a perception of unification and willingness to work as a team.

Sometimes those rules will be in the favor of the children. For example you may be giving them a later bed time or curfew due to being responsible and getting older. Others may tighten the reigns somewhat such as limiting TV or video game time. Divorced parents should never feel as if they have to be extremely lenient to win the affection of the children. Establishing very clear boundaries and rules for children is a very important part of keeping everyone happy. If you fail to do this then you will encounter many unneeded conflicts that continue over and over again.

Don't let Children Manipulate Divorced Parents

Divorce causes some children to play guilt-games or manipulate, disobey, rebel or act out. Children are inherently smarter than most of us give them credit for and they learn quickly what will annoy their parents. Most parents are very worried about how their divorce is going to affect their children. Some parents tend to give their children too much headway because they are worried about how they are affected by the divorce. Children tend to use manipulation after a divorce as a method of getting their way. Many parents fell as if the children are traumatized enough so they want to keep their environment striving and happy. Make every effort to stay firm with all established rules and guidelines and only make exceptions if the situations really warrants it, otherwise the children will feel as if you are letting them do what they want to do.

Don't be surprised if your children attempt to test the limits of the rules. This may be an indication that the children wants to live with the other parent. Make sure that similar rules exist at both homes. Children may encounter problems at school or otherwise; you need to understand these types of problems but you should never feel as if the divorce is a reason to ease up on the rules. The parents should find out what can be done to help work through the problems. Make sure you have an understanding between what your children need and when they are attempting to get something over on you. Parents should discipline and be firm, yet show sensitivity and understanding at the same time without letting their defenses down. Do not feel as if your children will not love you if you don't give into their desires.

Make Special Occasions Comfortable for Children With Divorced Parents

Special occasions should be made very comfortable for children after a divorce. You may determine that it is better to alternate and events like birthday parties at both homes. There will be some events that are not easily divided and that's where communication and compremise plays an important role. When children have special occasions like graduation, sporting events, dances, then both parents should be in attendance.Parents should not have any type of conflict with each other while attending these events and put the children in the position of having to choose one over the other to attend. Take under consideration that young children are deeply affected by this type of action.

Some newly divorced couples who are struggling with their own emotions of the divorce may have a hard time dealing with being in the presence of the ex-spouse. They should express to the child that it is difficult to see their other parent at the event are willing to give it a try. The parents should be focused on making the event a happy and lasting moment for the child. They may not want to hang out together at the event; however, they can treat each other with mutual respect. This portrays a good example of unity and teamwork for the children as well as other people. These types of situations will get much easier as time goes forward and the wounds have begun to heal from the divorce. This will happen if both parents made conscious effort and never allow foolish pride to get in the way.

Chapter 20: Can It Be That My Child Is A Victim Of Abuse?

It is very important for parents to touch base with their children as often as possible. Without sounding like a paranoid freak, let me say this, there is a lot that could go wrong in an hour's time; being away from your child any longer could mean unimaginable evils. But before you lose your mind and begin to embark on a fit-of-madness, also remember that THERE IS NOTHING YOU CAN DO TO KEEP YOUR CHILD SAFE 24/7.

Exercise:

Parents can try this exercise with their children just to try and see if all is well. This exercise is not meant to replace or represent any professional intervention/assistance your child might require. Let your child tick (√) next to the most appropriate statement on the RESPONSES column.

PROBABLE SCENARIOS: ....RESPONSES:

....Yes ....No

1. How are things between me and my mum/dad?

a)I usually find it easy to ask for stuff when ....a) ....a)
my mum/dad is happy than when s/he is in a bad mood.

b)When mum/dad is happy, it makes me happy ....b) ....b)
because s/he would not shout at me for no reason.

c) I know that each time my mum/dad is in a good ....c) ....c) mood, I will be treated to my favourite stuff.

d) Sometimes the person who scares me the most ....d) ....d)

is mum/dad because ...

e) I feel safer when mum/dad is at home because ....e) ....e)

2. When I am happy it means:

a) I often do most of my chores without being asked ....a) ....a)

to my mum/dad.

b) I often surprise my mum/dad by voluntarily ....b) ....b)

running errands and or chores.

c) That even my sibling/s would be taken care of ....c) ....c)

without me grumbling and complaining.

3. Relatives and extended family:

a) People like my uncle/aunt make me feel uncomfortable ....a) ....a) around them because ... (let the child explain if this is so).

b) Grandma/grandpa makes me uncomfortable by the things ....b) ....b) they say/do when mum/dad is not around or when we are alone in the house.

c) Sometimes grandma/grandpa or my uncle/aunt seem to be ....c) ....c) angry with me for no reason at all.

d) My ... (uncle/aunt/gran, etc.) likes to spend most of the time ....d) ....d) with me away from others.

e) My ... tells me not to tell others about the things we do ....e) ....e) together and s/he gives me nice things for not telling.

NB: Sometimes our relatives including our parents could still be harbouring unresolved feelings of resentment towards us and find it easy to express them on our children, particularly in our absence; so, do not simply dismiss things spoken by children about your folks, they could turn out to be true.

PROBABLE SCENARIOS: ....RESPONSES:

....Yes ....No

4. My body:

a) I know / (do not know) that my body belongs to me alone. ....a) ....a)

b) There is someone (or people) who makes me uncomfortable ....b) ....b) by the things he says (or does to) about my body.

c)I do not like it when others talk about my private parts it ....c) ....c) makes me feel ...

5. Keeping secrets:

a)Keeping secrets is not a bad thing because .... There are ....a) ....a)
things that I must keep secret.

b)People who wants me to keep secrets have promised to ... .b) ....b) if I keep the secret between us.

c)It is nice / not nice to keep a secret that makes me feel bad ....c) ....c) when I am keeping it.

d)I am keeping some things to myself because there is nobody ....d) ....d)
 who cares about me.

e)I am keeping the secret because I am afraid that ... .e) ....e) (let the child explain).

f) Yes I know (no, I do not know) what is a 'dirty little secret'. ....f) ....f)

6. At school:

a) There is a teacher who ....a)
...............a)

b) If I did not do my school work or home work I know that ... .b) ....b)

c) Everybody knows that I am Mr/Ms ... (teacher's name or ....c) ....c) surname) favourite pupil/learner.

d) Nobody knows that I am Mr/Ms ... (teacher's name or ....d) ....d) surname) favourite pupil/learner because ...

e) There are (there are no) secrets between me and Mr/Ms ....e)
..............e)

f) There are (there are no) secrets between me and some............f) ....f)
 kid named ...

g) Nobody takes my stuff including food without my ....g) ....g) permission at school.

h) Yes, some kid(s) take my stuff including food without my...........h) ....h) permission at school.

7. When I am next to … (mum/dad, grandma/grandpa, aunt/uncle, brother/sister, cousin) I sometimes feel:

a) Sick in the stomach. Maybe it is because ....a) ....a)

b) Like my hair is standing on its end......................b) ....b)

c) Like my heart beats fast......................c) ....c)

d) My legs wobble......................d) ....d)

e) My body shakes......................e) ....e)

8. My favourite person is …?

a) S/he is my favourite person because ....a) ....a)

b) The two of us have a secret no one knows about......................b) ....b)

c) S/he always makes me feel ....c) ....c) d)I like it when the two of us ……………………..d) ……………..d)

e)Our favourite chilling spot is ……………………..e) ……………..e)

f)Our favourite game is … [if the answer is "I cannot tell" ,……………..h) ……………..h)

you need to probe gently, same goes for e) here above.]

NB: Once the child tells any of the secrets, make sure that you assure

him/her that nothing would happen to them and truly take all

necessary steps to protect and prevent anything from happening.

But also make sure that you teach your child about the difference

between good and bad secrets and that the people who wants the

child to keep a bad or dirty little secret are the ones who are the bad

people and not the child.

If your family often attends religious gatherings where children are

exposed to individuals without your supervision, please probe into
things like routine activities and the related secrecy if any
just to be sure.

PROBABLE SCENARIOS: ....RESPONSES:

....
....................................Yes ....No

9. social media and its impact:

a) Things I like the most are ....a) ....a)

b) Things I dislike them most are ....b) ....b)

c) I have this friend or person who often ....c) ....c)

d) Some of my bad memories/ experiences in social media are ... .d) ....d)

e) The things which I saw in the internet and I never spoke to.......e) ....e) anybody about are ...

f) I was just curious when I saw ... so I decided to check it out............f) ....f)

g) I would not like my parent/s to find out about our...........g) ....g) conversations on social media because ...

h) When someone post/sends me pics, video clips or content...........h) ....h) I dislike I often ...

i) I have seen things on social media and internet which have...........i) ....j) made me ... (angry, disgusted, disappointed, unhappy, made my body feel very different especially my private part.)

j) I have / do not have pictures and video clips which I wish...........j) ....j) no one can see but me.

Chapter 21: The Importance Of Relaxation

When your child is feeling frustrated, upset, angry or simply overstimulated a proven idea to calm them down, is allowing them to try and relax. Knowing how to get your child to relax has many benefits such as reducing their heart rate, calming their emotions and allowing them to gather their thoughts and to think and respond from a place of calmness.

The relaxation I am talking about does not involve sitting in front of the tv either! A relaxation session or exercise can last from anywhere from ten minutes to one hour.

When someone feels stressed, their body responds with a physiological reaction known as the 'fight-or-flight' response. The body is responding to either a real or perceived danger, attack, or threat. Our muscles can become tense, our heart rate increases as does our breathing. We are ready to either take action (fight) or run away (flight). Even though this response occurs automatically, our bodies can get it wrong, as our brain does not know the difference between an actual real event or one that s made up in our mind. Try and get your child (and yourself too) in the habit of taking time out to relax. Getting your child to have a good night's sleep regularly, although a challenge, really has many benefits too, such as:

•Learning and memory. Research has shown that sleep can help the brain commit new information to a child's mind through memory consolidation.

•Mood. A sleep-deprived child may become irritable, impatient, lack concentration, and become moody. Sleep helps to reverse all of these effects, boosting your child's temperament.

•Metabolism and weight. Persistent sleep deprivation can alter hormones levels, affecting your child's appetite as a result.

•Cardiovascular health. Relaxation helps to combat chronic hypertension, reduce stress hormone levels, as well as maintain a regular heartbeat.

Try this simple progressive muscle relaxation exercise to help your child relax:

·Find a quiet and uninterrupted part of the house.

·Ask your child to get comfortable, whether that's sitting up in a chair or lying down.

·Get your child to close their eyes and focus on their breathing, inhaling and exhaling slowly and deeply.

·After five deep breaths, starting with their hands ask your child to clench both of their fists as tight as possible, clenching for fifteen seconds.

·After fifteen seconds ask your child to release their fists and get them to relax their entire body, for thirty seconds.

·Now its time to move to the next part of the body, and to continue this exercise in this order: face, shoulders, back, stomach, legs, feet and toes. Ask your child to tense and squeeze each of these body parts for fifteen seconds and then relax the body for thirty seconds, before moving on to the next body part.

·Complete this exercise by getting your child to shake out their body, removing all traces of tension.

Teaching Mindfulness

Mindfulness is a state of mind, focusing on the present moment. The here and now. Not thinking about yesterday or worrying about tomorrow. When you teach mindfulness to your child, it can help them combat negative thought patterns before the negative thoughts start to take over your child's life. Practicing mindfulness enables your child to develop self-awareness of both their inner and outer experiences. Mindfulness can help enhance your child's ability to calm down when they are distressed, help them to pay attention, as well as to make better decisions. As such, you should seek ways to introduce mindfulness into your child's daily life; it will help them to become aware of their body sensations, thoughts, feelings, and whatever it is that is happening externally and internally. An effective and popular mindfulness activity you can introduce to your child is the bell listening exercise:

•Bell listening exercise. (you will need a bell for this activity) Begin by getting your child into a comfortable position and ask them to close their eyes. Ring the bell, then ask your child to pay close attention to the vibration of the ringing sound. Request that they keep quiet and to remain silent and to focus on the sound of the bell. When your child can no longer hear the sound of the bell, ask them to raise their hand. Now get your child to continue with their eyes closed, and for the next sixty seconds get them to focus and listen out for any other noises that they hear. It could be the sound of a neighbour mowing the lawn, birds chirping, the dishwasher running, etc. This fun and simple exercise allows your child to stay in the present moment and to pay attention to their current experience. This exercise can be repeated numerous times.

Chapter 22: Be A Good Listener And Let Your Child Tell Their Side

Talking with our kids can be very daunting at times. A way to eliminate the standoff of them thinking we don't listen to them or us feeling they do not listen is to be a good listener and let your child tell their side. A good parent is a good listener with well developed communication skills. You need to acknowledge their feelings and give value to their viewpoints or opinions. Make sure to sit down with your kids and take the time necessary to listen with an open mind so they feel they are being heard.

When we first discover our kids have done something that is less then admirable we have a natural action to want to react when we should be thinking how we are going to respond. By responding instead of reacting we send a message to our kids that we are open to understanding all of their emotions and feelings. This allows them to tell their side of the story without any fear of what is going to happen to them for what they have done. If we fall into the trap of reacting we send our kids the wrong message that what they are feeling is not valid.

Determining why they feel the way they do can be accomplished with more questions and conversation so they can discuss their feelings further. This also opens up the opportunity to come up with a plan of action for a good solution to the situation that they may not otherwise think of on their own. Your kids will also be keenly aware that you do have an understanding of how they feel.

This is a situation that warrants giving your kids your complete attention. Make sure to remove all your distractions like reading the paper or watching television. This will allow you to hear their side of the story with a little side lesson in respect. Make sure to have good eye contact with your kids and be in control of the situation while offering possible solutions to the problem.

Do not make the mistake of discouraging your kids to not express their emotions. Respect their frustrations of feeling anger or being upset. When they are upset our first tendency is to try to do something to move them away from all that they are feeling, which could be a tactical parenting disaster. Asking questions to understand why they are having these feelings can go a long way in eliminating them.

Chapter 23: Keep Promises

Children would always love to hear when their parents promise them something and could always hate them most when they failed to keep such promises.In parenting, it is important that parents must do their part too and respect their children as well.

Keeping promises for their children is one way of showing that they respect and value their children.Children in return will also develop a sense of strong bond with their parents who could keep what they promised.It could be most difficult for the children to know that their parents have forgotten what they have promised to them.This could also be one reason why they rebel and become more difficult to handle.It could be difficult for the parents to keep their promise especially if they are too busy.

However, if they only think of the goodness of their children, they would never make promises to them that they could not keep.The children would never forget anything promised to them and would be more rebellious once their parents failed to do what they have been promised.The following suggestions could help how parents could keep their promises to their children.

Time management.Parents must learn to manage their time for work, for other work-related activities, house chores, and children.Parents who can manage their time well have ample time with their kids.Planning their schedules ahead of time could be of great help so that when they need to be with their kids they must not have work-related issues coming up to cancel it.

Prioritizing.Parents who prioritize their kids more than their other things have successful children.Children would be too happy to know that their parents prioritize them more than their careers, thus, they would never do anything to hurt their parents.However, once the children could sense that they are least in their parents' priority list that could be the time that they could be disrespectful and hard to handle.

Honesty.Children could well understand their parents if they could not keep their promise to them if they only explain and be honest enough to talk it over the reasons.

Compromising.Parents must know how to compromise their lost promises.They should not insist to their children that what they did could be good for them as well since they would never understand such point of view.Parents who know how to negotiate well with their children regarding their broken promises could always have a happy life with their kids.

Compensate.Parents should also know how to compensate the promises that they broke.Compensation could be in many other forms, one could be an instant treat to a favorite restaurant of the children, a new toy, a new dress, and many others.However, parents must see to it that the compensation they have could not look like bribery for the kids.Though it could help ease the pain that their children must be feeling, but they should see to it that the next time they promise something to their kids they should already keep it.

Thank you again for downloading this book!

I hope this book was able to help you to know how to instill a positive mindset in your child and to help them become strong, responsible individuals who achieve their goals.

The next step is to start by spending time with your children then from there you can know your child's talents, gifts, fears and ambitions and help them be the person they want to be.

Thank you and good luck!

Chapter 24: Talking To Kids About Divorce

One of the toughest things that most parents report through the divorce is having to actually sit down and discuss the divorce with your child. Many older kids may be aware that there was some stress in the family and may be expecting the divorce and they may be less surprised or angry about the decision. Typical questions that kids may have when Mom and Dad talk about divorce include:

- ☐ Why are you doing this?
- ☐ Don't you love each other anymore?
- ☐ Where will I live?
- ☐ When will I get to spend time with the other parent?
- ☐ What does divorce mean?
- ☐ Do you hate each other?
- ☐ Do you still love me?
- ☐ What am I supposed to tell my friends?
- ☐ How will this change my life?

Answering these questions and providing security, reassurance, love and support for your child or children is essential at this time and in the ongoing conversations you are likely to have with them about divorce.

HOW MUCH INFORMATION IS TOO MUCH

Ideally parents need to sit down together and decide what information they wish to share with their children with regards to the divorce. Generally kids need to know only what directly applies to them that would include:

- ☐ Where they will live
- ☐ How often and when they will see both parents
- ☐ That both parents still love the children, care for them and will be part of the children's lives on an ongoing basis
- ☐ Any changes that may occur in their home/school/ extracurricular activities
- ☐ Lifestyle changes (e.g. eating out once a week instead of all the time) Kids do not need to know and should not be told:

- ☐ Why the other person is a bad spouse/ parent/ partner
- ☐ Any negative feelings, thoughts or opinions about the other parent
- ☐ What part other people may have had in the divorce (affairs, new relationships, etc)
- ☐ Intimate details of the divorce
- ☐ Financial disclosures that are beyond the basics
- ☐ Child support payment information
- ☐ Character flaws of the other parent

Older children may ask more adult type questions, but it is still important to not get involved in being negative or "bashing" the other parent. Not all questions that children ask can or should be answered if the only way to answer is a negative. Kids will want an answer; however it will only cause more harm and further place the child in the middle of the conflict by providing this information. If you are consistent in your answers children will soon understand that you are not going to talk about the intimate or negative details of the divorce and will feel less conflicted about the other parent.

DISCUSSING DIVORCE

If at all possible kids should have the opportunity to discuss the divorce with both parents, together. This ensures that the children and the parents are hearing all the information and providing consistent information to the children. If kids get mixed information from Mom and Dad this will increase anxiety and confusion throughout the process.

Sometimes a family therapist, religious leader, counselor or even a family member can help as a mediator or advisor to the family to have these difficult conversations. The worse case scenario is to not have the discussion at all, which really does leave the children confused and highly stressed.

Reading a book about divorce with your child can also help. Check with your librarian or school counselor for a list of books on divorce written specifically for children.

ACTIVE LISTENING

Active listening is a critical skill in communication. It is the process of using all your powers of observation as well as your actual hearing to understand what the other person is really saying and meaning. Active listening is critical with kids that may not be able to express themselves with words. Watch for signs of stress, anxiety and distraction when talking about divorce that may indicate that the child is not ready or willing to hear and absorb the information.

Parents that use active listening skills will:

- ☐ Talk to the child in a comfortable, distraction free environment for the child

- ☐ Turn off the TV, cell phone, pager, computer, headset or other devices and just focus on the child

- ☐ Encourage communication and allow the child to express what they feel, even if it is not what you want to hear

- ☐ Ask nonjudgmental questions for clarification and more information
- ☐ Never criticize the child or make them feel unimportant
- ☐ Validate the child's feeling and clarify their misunderstandings or questions in a gentle, supportive way

FUTURE FOCUSED

Staying future focused and ending conversations about future goals will really help your children, although they need time in the conversation to talk about the past and the now. Talk about Mom and Dad's relationship with the children and how it can grow and improve and stay positive about the future. Kids will take their cues from how parents are acting, talking and confirming, so set a positive example when you have a conversation with your child.

Allow children to have some input as to their life in your home. Kids love to be involved in planning and activities, so use this as a way to engage them in their time with you at your house. Instead of talking about the past, look towards the future and new traditions and activities you all can enjoy together.

Chapter 25: Smart Kids Are Adaptable

Adaptability is cultivating our unique blend of multiple intelligences to give us choices for resolving the problems we face. This means being goal-oriented, but also having a respect for different ideas and versatility in problem-solving.

If there's anything that's guaranteed other than death and taxes, it's change. In the space of 50 years we've experienced more changes than in the previous 150; and in some cases, more changes in the last 10 years than in the last 50. Computers have gone from being room-sized and slow, to being hand-held and very fast in just the past 30 years. I recently observed a 5-year-old zipping through games on his I-Phone – games with plots and languages that I don't understand!

Jobs that were readily available 40 years ago are no longer there because of technological innovation, and new jobs have been created as a result of other innovations. Many years ago I visited a Boeing Fabrication Plant in Washington, and observed one person run a house-sized machine that took the place of 13 former metal-workers. Lost jobs, with no promise of other similar jobs to take their place; but a whole new world of tech-oriented jobs that were yet to be named.

We live in a global world now – where Spanish, French and Latin were once the foreign languages of choice, schools now have Japanese, several dialects of Chinese, German, Arabic and Thai. While discrimination is still there in varying degrees, the fact is that there are more and more children and young adults of mixed heritage in race, language, and ethnicity; which has deep implications for our economy and culture.

The earth is also rapidly changing, as demonstrated by melting glaciers, loss of marine and animal species, and more unpredictable weather. We fret that our schools and communities and government institutions haven't changed rapidly enough, and we may be right.

But the answers do not lie in debating the value or efficacy of America's educational model versus those in Finland or Japan or Germany. Those societies have much more centralized control over their schools than we do, for one thing. And for another, by the time the politicians and pundits come to any type of resolution for the rest of us, your children will be grown and on their own.

This is not to say that our schools can't, or don't need to, improve – they can and they do. But it does mean that we (parents and kids) need to stop pointing the finger at someone else – schools, politicians, the government – as the culprit that causes all our problems; and start doing the things we need to do, and can do, now.

MULTIPLE INTELLIGENCES

We all know that some kids are highly coordinated and great at sports, while others have more interest in the visual arts or in building something. Jason is highly coordinated, and loves all things physical, while David loves to read and Jill loves to talk and play with groups of people – whether friends or adults. There does appear to be some basis for genetic capabilities in each of us, although they're not totally understood.

Howard Gardner was perhaps the first psychologist to propose a theory of multiple intelligences; and he names eight of them – musical-rhythmic, visual-spatial, verbal-linguistic, logical-mathematical, bodily-kinesthetic, interpersonal, intrapersonal, and naturalistic. Other experts have added to this another dimension – that of existential-moral intelligence. These are not stand-alone skills – each of us has a unique blend of each of them, and not everyone will exhibit strong indicators of any specific 'intelligence.'

Here are brief descriptions of each type of intelligence:

Musical-Rhythmic:
Appreciation/orientation to rhythm and pitch. When hearing music, a child may pause and listen longer and with more concentration than others their own age.

Visual-Spatial: Able to think in images and pictures, and to visualize abstractly. May show up as responding to colors, and perhaps beginning to draw at an early age.

Verbal-Linguistic: Sensitivity to sounds, meaning and rhythm of language. May show well-developed verbal skills, picks up other languages easily and quickly.

Logical-Mathematical: Able to think conceptually and abstractly. May easily understand numerical patterns, logical explanations, and problem analysis – this is more readily observable around 3 years of age.

Bodily-Kinesthetic: Well coordinated, has excellent control of body movements, and easily manipulates objects. Demonstrates both small and large-motor coordination skills.

Interpersonal: Outgoing and gregarious; sensitive to moods and desires of others, and responds appropriately. Works well in groups.

Intrapersonal: Introverted and reserved, appears to be shy and a loner. In tune with their own feelings, beliefs, and thinking processes and seemingly less interested in others.

Naturalistic: Predisposition to nature – plants, animals, other natural objects.

Existential-Moral: Focused on deep questions of human existence and meaning of life. Moral awareness appears to begin developing around 2 years of age.

We all have different preferences and capabilities in these areas, and they're not always easily observable. But some children will show certain preferences early on, whether it's an overt response to music, being very physically active, or having a reserved personality that is seemingly focused on internal thoughts.

Many musicians and artists begin demonstrating extraordinary skill as children, as do some athletes. These abilities are only tendencies – they don't mean that some children are smarter than others just because they learn how to read or to multiply earlier than other children. The trick for parents is observing and supporting these preferences, but also encouraging their children to expand skills in other areas.

Skills of Adaptability. The more we expand our individual intelligences, the more adaptable we become in dealing with the diversity of our lives. How well a child adapts, or not, in any particular situation may depend not only upon the strength of his/her preferences; but also on what other skills they've learned that don't come quite as naturally. All of us want our kids to be versatile and resourceful in managing their lives.

For example, a child may be very self-focused and introspective; but it's essential that even shy, reserved children develop basic interpersonal skills so they can get along with other people in groups, and in work situations. And while some of us may prefer to focus on music or drama, we still have to be logical and analytical in other areas of our lives.

The value of understanding our intellectual capabilities in these ways is to fully appreciate the depth and breadth of what we call 'intelligence,' and to know that each of us has unique skills that we need to value on an equal basis.

Musical talents and interpersonal skills are not measured by IQ tests – which only measure verbal-linguistic and logical-mathematical domains – but IQ is routinely thought of as a statement of overall intelligence. Too many children, and adults, have learned to focus too much on their IQ score at 2nd grade as defining their level of intelligence.

Another advantage in knowing about multiple intelligences is understanding that every child is different, and will learn different skills at different rates. In fact, an introspective child may have a better understanding (or comprehension) of words than a child who simply sight reads, or spouts off multiplication tables by rote memory.

This should help all parents to relax a little when Jason doesn't read by age 3 (like Jill); but when he does learn to read, he may develop a higher level of reading comprehension more quickly.

Versatile Problem-Solvers. Adaptable people are versatile and resourceful, even adventurous; and are creative and imaginative in problem-solving – there is more than one way to move that rock. They pay attention to their surroundings, and develop a healthy competitiveness in dealing with it. They are ambitious self-starters, goal-oriented and enterprising. Experiencing different ways of doing things also enhances adaptability to unfamiliar situations.

A recent winner of a national high school science award felt he wasn't any smarter than anyone else; but, throughout most of his school years, he had spent many hours in the basement experimenting with all kinds of projects, "failing through" to success. Part of adaptability is also knowing that one failure is only one failure, that there are often many different ways to accomplish the same task; and being open to new ways of doing things. Businesses that expect to survive must also be adaptable to changing conditions and situations, both in terms of creativity and industry intelligence.

The opposite of adaptability is rigidity – "my way or the highway" – and resistance to new or different ideas and ways of doing things. Some children develop a hyper-competitive attitude, one where they tend to put others down to build themselves up; and they may engage in unreasonable risk-taking or dangerous behavior. Helping them focus on the problem at hand, rather than judging themselves and others as being "smart" or "not smart," will help.

Respect for Others. Kids that are adaptable have a respect for others, their ideas and opinions — and they have learned this by being respected themselves. They've learned to take turns, listen to another's ideas, and do what the group is doing even though it's not their favorite activity. They also learn that the ideas generated by two or more people in a group are sometimes more creative and better than just their idea; and they learn to collaborate, adjust and go with the flow.

David may prefer a very ordered, routine and repetitive environment because it makes him feel safer; but not all situations are controlled, so being exposed to a free-flow creative activity — while it makes him uncomfortable — is a critical skill for continued success. And Jason, with his mercurial personality, still needs to know when to stand in line and follow the rules so he can make similar judgment calls later in life.

Goal-Oriented. Helping kids focus on the end goal, or purpose, is critical; which means that adults need to make learning relevant to their interests and capabilities. Learning a skill in isolation is not only non-productive, but also non-motivating; so making the connection between math problems and everyday situations is essential – making change, figuring out how much allowance needs to be saved to purchase a toy truck, or measuring a patio to decide where to place a new outdoor rug.

Story problems in the classroom help; but children need you to reinforce those skills in everyday, hands-on activities so they can understand how to transfer information from one place to another to make them real – otherwise, story problems remain just stories.

The answers for you and your children, as for everyone else's, are with you as the most significant influence during the first five years of life. Parents create the setting for emotional maturity – love and self-esteem – while teachers are trained to specifically work with social and intellectual needs.

Your children – David, Jill and Jason – are all very different, even with the same parents, the same routines, the same school and community. And no one influences the architecture of their brains more than you. By the time they reach school, many of the most productive years of their brain development are gone – either used well, or frittered away because "...kids are just kids."

Learning how to be ADAPTABLE can be accomplished by:

Model flexibility – if you are flexible rather than frustrated at an unexpected event, then children learn to be flexible and tolerant as well.

Encourage their curiosity about the world, even if it puts them "off task" for a while. You never know when going off on a tangent will result in a sudden leap of understanding.

Establish basic boundaries that allow for flexibility – such as always having dinner at the same time, but flexing when you're going to a movie or the library.

Teach them to respect differences – different ideas, different cultures, different talents – which will expand their world of ideas.

Maintain a focus on the end goal, with the idea that there may be several ways to reach that goal. Don't simply let them, or yourself, off the hook.

Resolve tensions by taking unexpected happenings in stride, rather than being angry and placing blame.

Push them to try things they're not comfortable with – as long as it's safe and appropriate – and if they fail, to try again in a different way.

Praise them for making the effort, and having the courage to try.

Chapter 26: Prevent Childhood Illness With The Help Of Your Doctor

Children suffer from many illnesses, from the common cold and flu viruses to conjunctivitis and more.Teaching your child good hygiene practices, in addition to bring your child to the doctor for at least annual checkups, can ensure that your child's body is growing strong and healthy.Though your child probably hates going to the doctor, it is important that he/she becomes comfortable with the idea of getting checked regularly by a professional in order to ensure long-lasting health.

A doctor can monitor a child's height and weight, run blood tests, and make certain that the heart and lungs are clear and functioning properly.In addition, if your child is suffering from any ailment whatsoever, the sooner you can bring him/her to the doctor, the sooner he/she can receive the proper treatment for recovery. In this way, your child will be back at school sooner, and will not be risking the health of other children through the spreading of germs either. Bringing your child to the family physician from a young age can reduce the fear and anxiety that most children feel when they need to go to the doctor, because your doctor can develop a strong and friendly relationship with your child, easing his/her fears and making him/her comfortable during the examination. Your child will more readily open up about discomfort, pain, and other symptoms he/she may be feeling, which is also an added bonus to bringing your child to the doctor regularly. You can also catch diseases early on, before they cause serious problems, with annual physical exams.

The Benefits of Involving Your Children in Your Kitchen

Part of teaching children about healthy diets and the right foods to eat for sustained health and energy is getting them into the kitchen.Whether you let your children simply watch you prepare meals properly or if you choose to let them be actively involved in the cooking process, they will learn so many lessons about food preparation that they can take with them into adulthood.

Teach your children the proper ways to sanitize your kitchen environment, as well as how to properly clean fruits and vegetables prior to cooking them.In this way, they will understand that there are certain bacteria that can be found on foods, so you need to clean them well and cook them properly to get rid of the harmful bacteria before you eat the food.

Consider preparing meals with your children, whether it is pancakes at breakfast, sandwiches at lunch, or soups at dinner.A fun activity for children is helping their parents with desserts, such as creating a cookie or cake batter and then spooning it out or pouring it into a cake pan, and then watching the liquid batter transform into a solid cookie or cake while in the oven.

From learning about nutrition to learning about cooking tools, children will love spending time in the kitchen with you, and you can use this valuable time to bond and teach them well.When they are older, they can come up with their own recipes and you can try them together as well.

A word of warning; always closely supervise children while they are in the kitchen.

Ways to Teach Children about Dental Health from an Early Age

Dental health is extremely important, and children need to be taught about how to keep their mouths healthy and clean from a young age, in order to instill good habits and to understand why it is important to brush and floss daily.Children need to understand that, in addition to cavities, which require painful dental treatments, good oral hygiene can prevent serious infections from occurring in the mouth and spreading to other parts of the body.

Teach your children how to brush their teeth starting at about the age of 2, and make sure you train them in the proper brushing technique, which is in a circular motion as opposed to side-to-side. Also, be sure that your child understands that it is harmful to swallow the toothpaste and so it must be spit out completely prior to rinsing the mouth out with clean water. Utilize a child's toothbrush that he/she is comfortable with, and when he/she is older, you could consider introducing a motorized electric toothbrush that may be even more effective at keeping teeth clean.

Remember to teach your children to floss daily, in addition to using mouthwash to freshen breath and kill germs between teeth. Get them to understand that gum health is just as important as dental health, and brushing, flushing, and using mouthwash are good ways to keep gums strong and healthy. Establish a dental cleaning routine each morning and before bed, so that your child gets used to the routine and it becomes second nature.

Chapter 27: Identify Your Triggers

I find it uncomfortable identifying my triggers. I don't like looking into my own weakness. But doing so can help turn them to strengths – or at the very least stop them controlling your day. Write down the things that just make your blood boil and may cause you to explode, if you feel up to it, also identify ways to manage them.

Set the Scene

You've heard of 'fake it till you make it', right?

This works on that principle.

I went to a blessingway for an expectant friend once, and she asked us all to write down affirmations for her on post-it notes, and stick them all over the house, wherever we think they would suit. There were post-it notes with affirmations about her labour and life with the baby everywhere. Months later, they were still there because they made her feel strong every time she saw them.

Affirmations are valuable.

If you're religious, Bible verses would work well. If you're not, positive thoughts and statements that mean something to you will suit you. Stick them on the mirror, by the toilet, on the fridge, on the coffee jar.

Tell yourself this will get better. Tell yourself you are a good parent. Tell yourself it's okay to be sad/angry/hurt, but not to let that consume you. Tell yourself all the things you wish someone else was standing next to you saying.

You'll be surprised how quickly you begin to believe it.

Activity 8: Set the Scene

List as many affirmations as you need. Choose the ones you like best and write them on post-it notes or pretty paper. Place them in visible places around your living space. Be conscious about reading them whenever they catch your eye.

Set Up For Success

Tragedies don't normally come with warnings, so this particular point isn't always relevant. I'm not suggesting you fill the freezer with food when you've just heard bad news.

There are times, however, that giving yourself a helping hand is possible. For example, I know my mother's birthday is at the start of April. I know that in the week or so leading up to her birthday, I am going to find it harder to be enthusiastic. I'm going to have less appetite, I'm going to need a bit more peace around me than usual.

Without going into a tailspin, I can pop an extra portion or two of food in the freezer during March. I can prepare extra worksheets for the children, plan a few play dates, arrange to see something beautiful during the week that I know I'm likely to need some emotional support.

That's easily said when you know you can plan ahead. But what happens when it's all just too much, and you wake up one morning feeling like the world is on your shoulders?

Then you need to return to your categories, and break down what you need. The children need lunch – pack it the night before. Lay out clothes for them and give them the chance to dress themselves. Wash the dishes before going to bed, so that you don't have that overwhelm to deal with in the morning.

Whatever it is that will help you feel more positive in the morning, do it. Give yourself a fighting chance to make tomorrow better.

Do it every day, and soon it will become a habit too.

There are times when this involves making small changes. The thought of spending an hour at the end of a busy day washing dishes leaves me feeling like a servant rather than a mother. So instead, I have set myself little challenges: while the kettle is boiling, I empty the dish rack. I wash dishes during the 11-minute spin cycle or my washing machine. This massively reduces the post-dinner chore at the end of the day. You could use that time to stack the dishwasher. Or sweep the floor — whatever it is that makes later or tomorrow a little bit easier.

Set yourself small challenges, with easy to win targets that leave you feeling like you're making progress.

Small changes, big rewards. When life weighs heavily on you, these small victories can go a long way to keeping you afloat. Making your day-to-day that little bit more routine makes the tough days that little bit easier to pull through- and that's advice coming from someone with a strong aversion to routines!

Chapter 28: Start Parenting More Effectively

1. Decide What You Want to Work on First:

One of the things parents say is that they don't know where to start. But it is simple: start with the things that put your child at risk. These are the behaviors that are physically or emotionally dangerous to your child or others— where he is hurting somebody physically, breaking things, or being unsafe outside of the home.

If you want to change everything at once, you're going to be very disappointed. Not only is that an impossible task; you're going to alienate your child. Parents should address the things that violate their values and morals, and that are risky to the child and others. Start there.

2. Pinpoint Exactly What You Want to Change:

It is helpful for parents to break behaviors down into separate pieces and work on them one at a time. So if your child curses at you and storms up to his room and slams the door, start with the behavior you want to change most. When you talk with him, you want to break it down. Begin with, "Don't curse. That doesn't help solve the problem, and I'm offended by it. What do you think you could do differently the next time you get upset?" Your child may not be able to come up with anything, but offer some suggestions and get him to pick one option. And then say, "All right, so the next time you're upset, instead of cursing, you'll just go to your room."

So work on the behavior you want to change most— then, move on to the next one. Don't try to tackle everything at once.

3. Explain the Change:

If you're going to change a specific response to a behavior, it might be helpful to sit down with your child and explain what that change is going to be. When things are going well and everybody is calm, you can say, "Oh, by the way, I wanted to tell you something. Being grounded in your room all day when you use bad language is working around here. It doesn't seem to be helping you to change. So from now on when you curse, you're going to go into your room until you write a letter of apology. Then, when you're done with that letter, you can read it to me and we'll talk about it. While you're in your room, I'm going to take your computer and cell phone away to make sure you stay on target." Be clear on what you're going to do. Your child may get angry and frustrated, but don't let him turn it into an argument. Say, "I understand that it might be frustrating, but this is how I want our family to work."

4. Tell Your Child What the Goal Is:

Ii is important to define your goals to your child. You can say something like, "My goal is that you don't hurt other people by saying bad words." Or "My goal is that you don't steal money out of my wallet," or "My goal is that you don't punch the wall," or "My goal is that you don't throw sand in kids' faces or bite them when you're playing in the sandbox." You can start out the conversation by saying, "I've noticed that when somebody teases you a little, you get really upset and you get yourself into trouble. I hate to see that, because then you get punished— and it happens all over again the next day. So from now on, let's figure out a way for you to handle this differently so that you don't get into trouble. When someone teases you, what can you do instead?" And come up with a game plan of what he might do next time.

It's important to realize that what comes out of your mouth doesn't always get into your child's ear the way you want it to. And so even if your child is confused when you talk with him— he may be frustrated, worried, or angry— just try to stay calm. Whatever it is, say, "Let's just see how it works out first." Your child doesn't have to agree; it's not a democracy. But it's a way of approaching problems that, over time, will change his perceptions of his relationship with authority— and his relationship with you.

5. Manage Opportunity:

If you're concerned that your child is going to do something hurtful or destructive, one of your options is to manage the opportunities he has. Let's say you have a teenager who continuously gets speeding tickets. He doesn't respond to your efforts to get him to take responsibility and drive more safely. One of the things you can do is take away his car. When you do that, you're taking away the opportunity. It's similar with younger kids. If they demonstrate that they won't stop stealing money out of your wallet, take away the opportunity by putting a lock on your door or locking your purse in the trunk of your car. Opportunity management is one of the simplest ways of shaping behavior. In other words, if your daughter can't handle the mall without throwing tantrums, don't take her to the mall. If your son is at a restaurant and he can't stop acting out, take him out of the restaurant. Once your child demonstrates that he can't handle something, remove the opportunity until he shows you that he can. Often, if your child doesn't have the opportunity to do something, it won't happen.

6. Don't Appeal to Your Child's Empathy:

Asking your child, "Do you know how it feels when you're disrespectful to me?" or asking, "How do you think Tommy feels when you take his lunch money?" are appeals to your child's empathy. But children, and especially teenagers, don't experience much empathy for anybody. They are simply not in touch with those feelings. The apparatus that manages empathy in the mind is not working properly yet; some say it isn't fully formed. Regardless of the reasons, empathy is not an approach that will convince your child of anything. Consequently, they don't experience empathy for everyday situations, so you can't depend on that tactic to change their behavior. Instead, you have to work with their self-interest. If you want your child to change something, you have to demonstrate that he will benefit from changing; that it's in his self-interest. If you want your child to stop lying or manipulating, you have to frame it in a way so he can see how he would benefit from stopping that behavior. It's not helpful to say "Can't you see how much your manipulating hurts me?" Instead, say, "Aren't you sick of getting grounded for manipulating? You're the one who gets hurt when you manipulate. Remember, Josh, the consequences won't stop until the manipulation stops. So stop doing this to yourself."

7. Set Limits and Give Consequences:

An important component of teaching our kids is learning how to set limits on them. That's what your consequences should be designed to do. Accordingly, we can't make our child change. But if we use the right combination of consequences and motivation, we can, in a sense, make them thirsty to change.

Conclusion

Let's be honest, being a parent is the most rewarding job, but it can be extremely difficult at times. Throughout this eBook, I have shown you that parenting can be much easier and it is in your control. By focusing on putting in The Gap, creating awareness, having a roadmap to follow in the form of a parenting vision, you can make real changes in your life and the life of your child/ children. Recognize and remember that your children are learning. They don't know all the things that you expect them to know. Be patient, be kind, and be present in your parenting.

I am striving to be a better parent for my children and I want to help you to do the same. Having just completed writing this eBook, I was very quickly brought back to earth today with my parenting and received a gentle reminder that I needed to be "more present" to my children too. I picked up my eldest child to take her to an art class after school today. I had organized for my husband to pick up our other children, so I could have my one-on-one time with her. When she got in the car she said to me with a smile on her face "Mum you missed assembly today and I received a Principals Award. I kept looking for your face in the audience, but I couldn't find it." I said "I am so sorry".

I was mortified that I had missed it, I couldn't believe it. "But, I didn't know that there was an assembly today, I didn't even know you were getting an award" I replied.

"I told you during the week mum, but you were a bit distracted" she countered. "I said to myself when you weren't there that I knew you were really busy writing your eBook, so I needed to remember not to be too hard on you for forgetting". Out of the mouths of babes. A timely reminder to bring me back to the present and to be more present in my parenting!! Remember, there is no such thing as the perfect parent. You are doing the best you can with the resources that you have. The aim is to keep learning and be the best parent that you can be.

www.ingramcontent.com/pod-product-compliance
Lightning Source LLC
Chambersburg PA
CBHW072004070526
44583CB00015B/1327